PRAISE FOR **THE LONG HAUL**

"Exquisite. . . . Murphy can cross class boundaries as smoothly as changing lanes on the highway. . . . Readers even passingly familiar with the burgeoning literary genre we might call hillbilly elegiacs . . . will find Murphy's more nuanced perspective refreshing."

—Meghan Daum, *New York Times Book Review*

"*The Long Haul* delivers because it is a survey of a culture fused to a working man's memoir—and Murphy, smartly, avoids sentiment and lazy comparisons." —Jeffery Gleaves, *Paris Review*

"Like priests, movers shepherd us through life's transitions; like cowboys, truckers drive the roads we'll never know. Both see America in ways the rest of us don't. In *The Long Haul*, Murphy . . . bring[s] us into his semi-mythic world." —Joshua Rothman, *The New Yorker*

"An adventure story and . . . a peek into an occupation whose practitioners we see rolling down the highway."

—Jim Higgins, *Milwaukee Journal Sentinel*

"*The Long Haul* beguil[es] readers with wit, wisdom and observations born from decades in transit." —Jason Blevins, *Denver Post*

"Finn Murphy . . . bring[s] readers along for a rollicking ride through a trucker's world and [provides] an insider's eye, pairing it with an involving series of encounters." —*Midwest Book Review*

"[A]n inside look at the unglamorous life of a trucker. . . . Even if you have no aspirations to life on the open road, you'll enjoy this author's prose." —Jim Cameron, *Connecticut Post*

"If you've ever considered hiring a moving company to get you to a new home, pick this book up first to get insight into the people who are going to make it happen." —*East Oregonian*

"[Murphy] kept my interest the whole way through with his gritty, sometimes hilarious descriptions of the people he moved for and his observations about life on the road, other movers and trucking in general." —Dorothy Cox, *The Trucker*

"*The Long Haul* is one of those rare books that peeks inside an industry that the general public rarely ever hears about (except when bad stuff happens). . . . [R]eaders will be spellbound." —Terri Schlichenmeyer, *10-4 Magazine*

"Walt Whitman would've liked Finn Murphy's excellent book, *The Long Haul*. Pulling his dreams and burdens across the open road, Murphy weaves a soulful tapestry of America out of asphalt, diesel fuel, and human need." —Steve Dublanica, best-selling author of *Waiter Rant*

"A coast-to-coast ride that is trenchantly observed, wryly funny, and filled with human drama." —Tom Vanderbilt, best-selling author of *Traffic*

"It seems strange that American letters has not produced a trucker-writer—until now. If you ever wonder about these American nomads, their lore, their lives crisscrossing this land, pick up this book." —Ted Conover, best-selling author of *Newjack*

THE LONG HAUL

A TRUCKER'S TALES OF LIFE ON THE ROAD

Finn Murphy

W. W. NORTON & COMPANY

INDEPENDENT PUBLISHERS SINCE 1923

NEW YORK | LONDON

The Long Haul is a work of nonfiction. Certain names, identifying details, and locales have been altered.

For information about permission to reproduce selections from this book, write to Permissions, W. W. Norton & Company, Inc., 500 Fifth Avenue, New York, NY 10110

For information about special discounts for bulk purchases, please contact W. W. Norton Special Sales at specialsales@wwnorton.com or 800-233-4830

Manufacturing by LSC Communications, Harrisonburg
Book design by Daniel Lagin
Production manager: Beth Steidle

Library of Congress Cataloging-in-Publication Data

Names: Murphy, Finn, 1958– author.
Title: The long haul : a trucker's tales of life on the road / Finn Murphy.
Description: First edition. | New York, N.Y. : W W. Norton & Company, [2017]
Identifiers: LCCN 2016059479 | ISBN 9780393608717 (hardcover)
Subjects: LCSH: Murphy, Finn, 1958– | Truck drivers—United States—
Biography. | Trucking—United States—Anecdotes.
Classification: LCC HD8039.M7952 U55758 2017 | DDC 388.3/24092
[B]—dc23
LC record available at https://lccn.loc.gov/2016059479

ISBN 978-0-393-35587-1 pbk.

W. W. Norton & Company, Inc.
500 Fifth Avenue, New York, N.Y. 10110
www.wwnorton.com

W. W. Norton & Company Ltd.
15 Carlisle Street, London W1D 3BS

2 3 4 5 6 7 8 9 0

To my mother, Katherine Joan Byrne Murphy,
who taught me how to read.

To Pam, who hung in there all the way.

Freeways cars and trucks
Stars beginning to fade, and I lead the parade

—TOM WAITS, "OL' '55"

CONTENTS

PART III: **THE BIG SLAB**

INTRODUCTION

Loveland Pass, Colorado, on US Route 6 summits at 11,991 feet. That's where I'm headed, having decided to skip the congestion at the Eisenhower Tunnel. Going up a steep grade is never as bad as going down, though negotiating thirty-five tons of tractor-trailer around the hairpin turns is a bit of a challenge. I have to use both lanes to keep my 53-foot trailer clear of the ditches on the right side and hope nobody coming down is sending a text or sightseeing.

At the top of the pass, high up in my Freightliner Columbia tractor pulling a spanking-new, fully loaded custom moving van, I reckon I can say I'm at an even 12,000 feet. When I look down, the world disappears into a miasma of fog and wind and snow, even though it's July. The road signs are clear enough, though—the first one says RUNAWAY TRUCK RAMP 1.5 MILES. Next one: SPEED LIMIT 35 MPH FOR VEHICLES WITH GROSS WEIGHT OVER 26,000 LBS. Next one: ARE YOUR BRAKES COOL AND ADJUSTED? Next one: ALL COMMERCIAL VEHICLES ARE REQUIRED TO CARRY CHAINS SEPTEMBER 1—MAY 31. I run through the checklist in my mind. Let's see: 1.5 miles to the runaway ramp is too far to do me any good if the worst happens, and 35 miles per hour sounds really fast. My brakes are cool, but adjusted? I hope so, but no mechanic signs off on brake adjustments in these litigious days. Chains? I have chains in my equipment compartment, required or not, but they won't save my life sitting where they are. Besides, I figure the bad weather will last for only the first thousand feet. The practical aspects of putting on chains in a snowstorm, with no pullover spot, in pitch dark, at 12,000 feet, in a gale, and wearing only a T-shirt, is a prospect Dante never considered in enumerating his circles of hell. The other option is to keep rolling—maybe I'll be crushed by my truck at the bottom of a scree field, maybe I won't. I roll.

I can feel the sweat running down my arms, can feel my hands shaking, can taste the bile rising in my throat from the greasy burger I ate at the Idaho Springs Carl's Jr. (It was the only place with truck parking.) I've got 8.6 miles of 6.7 percent downhill grade ahead of me that has taken more trucks and lives than I care to think about. The road surface is a mix of rain, slush, and (probably) ice. I'm one blown air hose away from oblivion, but I'm not ready to peg out in a ball of flame or take out a family in a four-wheeler coming to the Rocky Mountains to see the sights.

I downshift my thirteen-speed transmission to fifth gear, slow to 23 mph, and set my Jake brake to all eight cylinders. A Jake brake is an air-compression inhibitor that turns my engine into the primary braking system. It sounds like a machine gun beneath my feet as it works to keep 70,000 pounds of steel and rubber under control. I watch the tachometer, which tells me my engine speed, and when it redlines at 2,200 rpm I'm at 28 mph. I brush the brakes to bring her back down to 23. If it's going to happen, it's going to happen now. My tender touch might cause the heavy trailer to slide away and I'll be able to read the logo in reverse legend from my mirrors. It's called a jackknife. Once it starts, you can't stop it. In a jackknife the trailer comes all the way around, takes both lanes, and crushes against the cab until the whole thing comes to a crashing stop at the bottom of the abyss or against the granite side of the Rockies.

It doesn't happen, this time, but the weather's getting worse. I hit 28 again, caress the brake back down to 23, and start the sequence again. Fondle the brake, watch the mirrors, feel the machine, check the tach, listen to the Jake, and watch the air pressure. The air gauge read 120 psi at the summit; now it reads 80. At 60 an alarm will go off, and at 40 the brakes will automatically lock or just give up. Never mind that now, just don't go past 28 and keep coaxing her back down to 23. I'll do this twenty or thirty times over the next half an hour, never knowing if the trailer will hit a bit of ice, the air compressor will give up, the Jake will disengage, or someone will slam on the brakes in front of me. My CB radio is on (I usually turn it off on mountain passes), and I can hear the commentary from the big-truck drivers behind me.

"Yo, Joyce Van Lines, first time in the mountains? Get the fuck off the road! I can't make any money at fifteen miles an hour!"

"Yo, Joyce, you from Connecticut? Is that in the Yewnited States? Pull into the fuckin' runaway ramp, asshole, and let some men drive."

"Yo, Joyce, I can smell the mess in your pants from inside my cab."

I've heard this patter many times on big-mountain roads. I'm not entirely impervious to the contempt of the freighthauling cowboys.

Toward the bottom, on the straightaway, they all pass me. There's a Groendyke pulling gasoline, a tandem FedEx Ground, and a single Walmart. They're all doing about 50 and sound their air horns as they pass, no doubt flipping me the bird. I'm guessing at that because I'm looking at the road. I'll see them all later, when they'll be completely blind to the irony that we're all here at the same time drinking the same coffee. Somehow, I've cost them time and money going down the hill. It's a macho thing. Drive the hills as fast as you can and be damn sure to humiliate any sonofabitch who's got brains enough to respect the mountains.

My destination is the ultrarich haven called Aspen, Colorado. This makes perfect sense because I'm a long-haul mover at the pinnacle of the game, a specialist. I can make $250,000 a year doing what is called high-end executive relocation. No U-Hauls for me, thank you very much. I'll take the movie stars, the ambassadors, the corporate bigwigs. At the office in Connecticut they call me the Great White Mover. This Aspen load, insured for $3 million, belongs to a former investment banker from a former investment bank who apparently escaped the toppled citadel with his personal loot intact. My cargo consists of a dozen or so crated modern art canvases, eight 600-pound granite gravestones of Qing Dynasty emperors, half a dozen king-size pillow-top beds I'll never figure out how to assemble, and an assortment of Edwardian antiques. The man I'm moving, known in the trade as the shipper, has purchased a $25 million starter castle in a hypersecure Aspen subdivision. He figures, no doubt accurately, he'll be safe behind the security booth from the impecunious widows and mendacious foreign creditors he ripped off, but I digress.

I'm looking downhill for brake lights. I can probably slow down, but there's no chance of coming to a quick stop. If I slam on the brakes I'll either crash through the vehicle in front of me or go over the side. I want to smoke a cigarette, but I'm so wound up I could never light it, so I bite off what's left of my fingernails. I'm fifty-eight years old, and I've been doing this off and on since the late 1970s. I've seen too many trucks mashed on the side of the road, too many accidents, and too many spaced out-drivers. On Interstate 80 in Wyoming I watched a truck in front of me get blown over onto its side in a windstorm. He must have been empty. On I-10 in Arizona I saw a state trooper open the driver door of a car and witnessed a river of blood pour out onto the road.

The blood soaking into the pavement could be mine at any moment. All it takes is an instant of bad luck, inattention, a poor decision, equipment failure—or, most likely, someone else's mistake.

If any of those things happen, I'm a dead man.

———

Those loud but lowly freighthaulers up on Loveland Pass would have mocked any big-truck driver going downhill as slowly as I was, but I've no doubt they were particularly offended because I was driving a moving van. To the casual observer all trucks probably look similar, and I suppose people figure all truckers do pretty much the same job. Neither is true. There's a strict hierarchy of drivers, depending on what they haul and how they're paid. The most common are the freighthaulers. They're the guys who pull box trailers with any kind of commodity inside. We movers are called bedbuggers, and our trucks are called roach coaches. Other specialties are the car haulers (parking lot attendants), flatbedders (skateboarders), animal transporters (chicken chokers), refrigerated food haulers (reefers), chemical haulers (thermos bottle holders), and hazmat haulers (suicide jockeys). Bedbuggers are shunned by other truckers. We will generally not be included in conversations around the truckstop coffee counter or in the driver's lounge. In fact, I pointedly avoid coffee counters, when there is one, mainly because I don't have time to waste, but also because I don't buy into the trucker myth that most drivers espouse. I don't wear a cowboy hat, Tony Lama snakeskin boots, or a belt buckle doing free advertising for Peterbilt or Harley-Davidson. My driving uniform is a three-button company polo shirt, lightweight black cotton pants, black sneakers, black socks, and a cloth belt. My moving uniform is a black cotton jumpsuit.

I'm not from the South and don't talk as if I were. Most telling, and the other guys can sense this somehow, I do not for a moment think I'm a symbol of some bygone ideal of Wild West American freedom or any other half-mythic, half-menacing nugget of folk nonsense.

Putting myth and hierarchy aside, I will admit to being immensely proud of my truck-driving skills, the real freedom I do have, and the certain knowledge that I make more money in a month than many of the guys around the coffee counter make in a year. The freighthaulers all know this, of course, and that's one reason bedbuggers aren't part of the brotherhood. It even trickles down to waitresses and cashiers. A mover waits longer for coffee, longer in the service bays, longer for showers, longer at the fuel desk, longer everywhere in the world of trucks than the freighthauler. It's because we're unknown. We don't have standard routes, so we can't be relied on for the pie slice and the big tip every Tuesday at ten thirty. We're OK with being outside the fellowship because we know we're at the apex of the pyramid. In or out of the trucking world, there are very few people who have what it takes to be a long-haul mover.

A typical day may have me in a leafy suburban cul-de-sac where landscapers have trouble operating a riding lawn mower, much less a 70-foot tractor-trailer. Another day may put me in the West Village of Manhattan navigating one-way streets laid

out in the eighteenth century. Long-haul movers don't live in the
rarified world of broad interstate highways with sixty-acre termi-
nals purpose-built for large vehicles. We've got to know how to
back up just as well blind-side as driver-side; we've got to know
to the millimeter how close we can U-turn the rig; and we've
really got to know that when we go in somewhere we can get out
again. A mundane morning's backup into a residence for a mover
will often require more skill, finesse, and balls than most freighthaulers might call upon in a year.

Since I now work for a boutique van line doing high-end executive moves, all of my work is what we call pack and load. That
means I'm responsible for the job from beginning to end. My crew
and I will pack every carton and load every piece. On a full-service
pack and load, the shipper will do nothing. I had one last summer
that was more or less typical: The shipper was a mining executive
moving from Connecticut to Vancouver. I showed up in the morning with my crew of five veteran movers; the shipper said hello,
finished his coffee, loaded his family into a limousine, and left for
the airport. My crew then washed the breakfast dishes and spent
the next seventeen hours packing everything in the house into
cartons and loading the truck. At destination, another crew
unpacked all the cartons and placed everything where the shipper
wanted it, including dishes and stemware back into the break-
front. We even made the beds. We're paid to do all this, of course,
and this guy's move cost his company $60,000. That move filled
up my entire trailer and included his car. It was all I could do to
fit the whole load on without leaving anything behind, but I managed it. I do remember having to put a stack of pads and a couple
of dollies in my sleeper, though.

How well a truck is loaded is the acid test of a mover. I can
look at any driver's load and tell at a glance if he's any good at all.

Drivers are always comparing themselves to other drivers and always learning new tricks from each other. Often when sitting around over coffee or beers, preferably not at a truckstop, we'll talk loading technique into the wee hours.

The basic unit of loading a moving van is called a tier. A tier is a wall of household goods assembled inside the van. My 53-foot moving van contains 4,200 cubic feet of space. Household goods average 7 pounds a cubic foot, so my truck can hold over 30,000 pounds. A standard tier is about 2 feet deep and goes across the truck 9 feet and up to the ceiling 10 ten feet, so a tier takes up 160 cubic feet. In a fully loaded van there will be twenty-five tiers each weighing 1,100 pounds, more or less.

When I arrive at a residence to begin a move, assuming I've gotten into the driveway and close to the house, the first thing I'll do is prep the residence. My crew and I will lay pads and then Masonite on any wood floors, carpets will be covered with a sticky durable film that gets rolled out, and we'll lay out neoprene runners throughout the house. Banisters and doorways will be padded with special gripping pads. Anything in the house that might get rubbed, scratched, banged, dented, or soiled is covered. Next, we'll go around with the shipper to see exactly what is going and what is staying. Then we'll pack everything in the house into cartons. I don't love packing; it's inside work and mostly tedious. I do enjoy packing stemware, china, sculpture, and fine art, but that stuff is getting rarer in American households. Books are completely disappearing. (Remember in *Fahrenheit 451* where the fireman's wife was addicted to interactive television and they sent fireman crews out to burn books? That mission has been largely accomplished in middle-class America, and they didn't need the firemen. The interactive electronics took care of it without the violence.)

After packing, which usually takes at least a full day on a full load, I'll write up an inventory where I put numbered stickers on everything that's moving and jot a short description on printed sheets. The numbers all get checked off at destination so we know everything we loaded has been delivered. The inventory includes not only a description of the item but also its condition and any marks or damage. It's essential for me to catalog the origin condition of an item in the event a shipper files a damage claim. A lot of criticism about movers has to do with how claims are handled. Moving companies require considerable documentation before paying a claim. Do you know why? It's because so many people file bogus claims. Lots of folks want to get the moving company to pay for a refinishing job on Aunt Tillie's antique vanity. Guess what? The moving company doesn't pay these types of claims, nor does some nameless insurance company. The driver pays them. Me, personally, out of pocket. My deductible is $1,600 per move. That's one reason why I'm going to be careful with your stuff, and it's also why I'm going to write up an accurate inventory.

After prep and packing, the crew will break down beds, unbolt legs from tabletops, and basically take anything apart that comes apart. Next we'll bring in stacks of moving pads and large rubber bands, and cover all the furniture. Padding furniture with rubber bands is a working-class art form. The bands are made by cutting up truck tire tubes into circles. Down south I'll often see an old black man sitting on a bench at a truckstop cutting up tubes with his knife and putting them into piles. Fifty bands go for five dollars.

Upholstered pieces like sofas will be padded and then shrink-wrapped. Nothing on any of my jobs will ever leave the residence unpadded. The whole point is to minimize the potential for damage, thereby minimizing the potential for a claim. Movers don't like claims. We don't like to get them, we don't like to deal with them, and we certainly don't like to pay them.

After all this preparation, I'll have a very clear idea how I'm going to load my truck. Smart drivers will always load problem pieces, called chowder, first. Chowder slows you down, takes up too much room, and is usually lightweight for the amount of space it takes up. Chowder also has a greater potential to damage goods loaded around it. Obviously I wouldn't load a leather sofa next to a barbecue grill. All drivers hate chowder, but it's a fact of life, and how you handle it is one of the things that separate good drivers from bad. The general loading rule is chowder first, cartons last.

Now I'm ready to start loading. I'll start my tier with base pieces like a dresser and file cabinets. On top of the base I'll load nightstands, small desks, and maybe an air conditioner. Now the tier is about eye level, with two rows of furniture going all the way across. The next level I'll load end tables, small bookcases, and maybe a few cartons to keep it all tight. The next level I'll lay some dining room chairs on their backs, starting with the armchairs and then interlocking the other chairs. Any open space in the tier gets filled with chowder like wastebaskets and small, light cartons. Now the tier is about eight feet high, and I'll be up on a ladder. The next level will be light, bulky things such as laundry hampers, cushions, and plant racks. At this point there will be a few inches open to the roof, and I'll finish the tier with maybe an ironing board and any other flat and light stuff I can find, like bed rails. When I'm finished I should have a uniform and neat tier from floor to ceiling with no gaps or open spaces anywhere.

A well-built tier is a beautiful thing to see and lots of fun to make. It's basically a real-life, giant Tetris game with profound physical exertion incorporated into the mix. When I'm loading I go into a sort of trance because I'm totally focused on visualizing everything in the house and mentally building tiers. This is one of the sweet spots where—as anyone who has done repetitive manual labor understands—the single-minded focus, concentration, and hard physical work combine to form a sort of temporary nirvana. Helpers who regularly work with the same driver will anticipate what piece the driver wants next before he even asks for it, and furniture will disappear into a tier the instant it's brought out. This makes loading go very quickly, and it resembles nothing so much as an elegant, intimate dance between crew and driver. Because I have a picture of everything in the house in my head, I'll often leave the truck to fetch a particular piece for a particular spot.

It's hard work. On a standard loading day I'll spend ten to fourteen hours either carrying something heavy, running laps up and down stairs to grab items, carrying furniture and cartons between the house and the trailer, and hopping up and down a double-sided stepladder building my tiers.

In addition to the mental and physical strain of packing, loading, and keeping my crew motivated, there is also the presence of the shipper. Shippers are frequently not at their best on moving day. They are, after all, leaving their home and consigning all their possessions over to strangers. Shippers can be testy, upset, suspicious, downright hostile, and occasionally pleasant and relaxed. It's the driver's job, in addition to loading and carrying, to make sure everything and everybody runs smoothly.

To put it all in a nutshell, the long-haul driver is responsible for legal documents, inventory, packing cartons, loading, claim prevention, unpacking, unloading, diplomacy, human resources, and customer service. The job requires an enormous amount of physical stamina, specialized knowledge, and tact. I am, as John McPhee called it, the undisputed admiral of my fleet of one.

My share of that Vancouver job came to around $30,000 for ten days' work. I had to pay the labor, of course, and my fuel and food. Still, I netted more than $20,000. A first-year freighthauler for an outfit like Swift or Werner won't make that in a year.

I guess that's worth being insulted in the mountains by my brethren.

———

The long-haul driver portrayed above is the kind of guy you want moving you. That's me, nowadays. There are lots of guys like me out there and lots of a different kind. I've been both. My own baptism into life as a driver for a major van line was not smooth. I was nervous and cocky when I first got on the road. Those might appear to be contradictory characteristics, but they are not for a twenty-one-year-old white American male from the suburbs who's operating way out of his element. Before I was taken on at North American Van Lines, I'd worked several summers as a local mover. I was known as a hard worker, which made me cocky, but was out on the road all alone, which made me nervous. I was consumed with getting the day's work done, getting the next load, and making the monthly revenue goals I'd set for myself. I was careless loading and unloading and extremely touchy with both shippers and helpers. I was in over my head. At the ripe old age of twenty-one I shouldn't have been doing that job, given my emotional maturity. The fact that I *was* there says a lot about the moving business. The industry will pretty much take anyone willing to do the work. I was willing enough, but lacking the other qualities that make for a good mover or a good truck driver. Almost forty years later, I am a calm, meticulous, and imperturbable driver. I am highly sought after and exorbitantly paid. That didn't happen overnight.

You're about to go out on the road with me, a long-haul mover. It's a road uncongested by myth. You'll see the work, meet the families I move, and visit with the people who populate this subculture. You'll smell the sweat, drink in the crummy bars, eat the disgusting food, manage an unruly labor pool, and meet some strange people. But I hope you'll also experience the exhilaration and the attraction, of the life . . . out there.

You'll also see what really happens behind the scenes when a family calls in the van line to pursue that all-powerful American imperative: The Next Big Thing. More than forty million Americans move every year. Careful people, who lock their doors, carry umbrellas, and install alarm systems, casually and routinely consign everything they own over to "the movers" without a second thought.

I find that a bit odd, don't you?

Come on, let's take a little ride.

PART I
THE TRUCK

Chapter 1
PUNCHING IN

'Ve lived a good part of my life in an odd netherworld. Working people are suspicious of my diction and demeanor, and white-collar people wonder what a guy like me, who looks and sounds like them, is doing driving a truck and moving furniture for a living. The truth is, I wasn't brought up to be a long-haul mover. I was raised by conscientious parents, educated by the Catholic Church, and fine-tuned by the sensibilities of a prestigious New England liberal arts college. None of it stuck because Dan Bartoli, the proprietor of Dan's Service Station in Cos Cob, Connecticut, where I got my first job, nailed me at an impressionable time and introduced me to low company and hard work.

Working at Dan's blasted me out of the sheltered, church-oriented life I had known. My baptism began the first instant of my first day at the gas station when Dan trotted out his employee orientation speech:

"The middle word of this enterprise is 'Service,' and that's what we give here. The first word of this enterprise is 'Dan's,' that's me. You give service and remember that this business belongs to me, we'll get along fine. You got that, you dim fuckin' peckerwood?"

Before that day I can't remember ever being sworn at. Before that day I had never heard an adult say the word "fuck." I was fifteen years old. Dan wasn't kidding about service. You had to wash all the windows, check the oil, the power steering fluid, the brake fluid, and the transmission fluid, wipe off any spilled gas, and chat up the customer about the latest Yankee game or town gossip, all in a fluid motion so as not to waste anyone's time but still give full value to each customer. Dan was a master. He knew every customer's name, their kids' names, and the latest news from the church, firehouse, Rotary meeting, or school. In public, Dan always had the perfectly appropriate response for any social situation. It was an elaborate ritual, and regular customers would stop and get two bucks' worth of gas just for the experience.

I don't know why, but I felt right at home. I liked being around machines and being taught how to use them properly. (My father couldn't distinguish the business end of a screwdriver from the handle.) I liked the responsibility too. It was a huge adolescent passage to be selected to work the night shift, from 6 to 9 p.m., because it meant I was a trusted member of the team. In my family, where the term "school night" had a religious ring and all social activities were proscribed, work was the one exception. Since I lived only a few minutes' walk away and was eager to find some solace from my seven brothers and sisters sequestered in a too-small house ruled by the iron fist of an Irish matriarch, I was a ready candidate for the night shift.

The idea now seems incredible that a lone fifteen-year-old boy would be placed in a gas station on US Route 1 at night, collecting cash, but it was a more innocent time. Dan's cash-management protocol was that whenever we had fifty dollars in the till we were to slip thirty into the safe and keep twenty for the bank. His instructions about what to do if we were robbed were unequivocal:

"Give the Bluegum all the money, fill up his stolen car, get the license plate, and call the cops. Even your measly life isn't worth twenty bucks to me." I was surprised that in Dan's world all thieves and drug users were black and from the Bronx. In my admittedly limited experience, theft and drug use were exclusive to Dan's own employees and the kids from the even more affluent Backcountry, who were all white, privileged denizens of Greenwich, Connecticut.

The other plum shift at Dan's was any weekday after four thirty. That's when the movers from Callahan Bros. Moving & Storage, located next door, would walk past the gas island and settle themselves along the steel median fence under the big tree at the far end of Dan's lot to drink beer after they'd punched out for the day.

All of Dan's gas jockeys were well acquainted with the Callahan men because we'd see them every day adding to the chain of beer can tops they'd been assembling for years between the trees. Building the chain of beer can tops was a sea change from the more ancient practice of simply throwing the empty cans up onto Dan's roof, which had been flat with a big lip all around. That tradition ceased when it was time for Dan to replace his roof, and rather than move several thousand beer cans, the roofers just laid new plywood over the cans and made the roof flush with what had been the lip. After this improvement, the cans simply rolled off, so it was time for a new game. That's when they started building the chain of beer can tops. At the time of my ascension from gas jockey to mover, the chain wound back and forth about six times along a distance of about sixty feet. I've no idea how many beers that represented, but I do know it wasn't a true sampling of consumption, because every once in a while Dan would get pissed off at the movers for pulling some stupid antic and he'd rip down the chain and ban them forever from beer drinking on his property. That meant things would resume their normal tempo the following Monday.

I knew John Callahan, owner of Callahan Bros., because every morning he would park his car at Dan's gas pump for one of us to fill the tank and check the oil. John would leave a quarter on the dashboard as a tip to whoever got to the car first. This would be, to my certain knowledge, the only Callahan Bros. vehicle whose oil level was ever regularly checked. The quarter was always an incentive for someone to stub out his smoke and service John's car. John's quarter wasn't nearly as big an incentive as the crisp new dollar bill that Griff Harris, the insurance man and former mayor, left on the steering wheel, though. Griff Harris always had the newest-model Cadillac Eldorado, and the gas jockeys would often fight to get to it more for the privilege of driving his car the fifty feet to his parking space than for the dollar. Griff's office was around the corner, and he and John Callahan constituted the summit of local royalty by being the only two people in Cos Cob who could drive up to the gas pumps and leave their car unattended without provoking a cataclysmic conniption from Dan.

Dan's gas jockeys were ardent observers of the Callahan men and their habits. As I got a little older and saw the movers crossing the gas island over to the tree, their green T-shirts soaking wet with sweat or brine-encrusted with dried sweat, pounding beers in the late-summer sun, telling their stories of hard work done well, hard work done poorly, road trips, good moves, horrendous moves, my interest intensified. The gas jockeys were part of their scene in a distant kind of way, but it was abundantly clear we were not part of their world. Like the Post Road in front, and Dan's next door, the gas jockeys were background music for the movers. We were younger, for one thing, and we didn't do the same kind of work, for another. Especially that kind of work which was a source of pride for them and awe for us. Lots of people simply *can't* do that kind of work, and we all wondered, if the day ever came, whether we would measure up and be dubbed "a good worker" or fail and be permanently dismissed as "candy-ass office muck." We could see the scars, smell the sweat, and translate the banter. This was tough work for tough men. Because of that, no gas jockey would have dreamed of approaching the movers, initiating a conversation, or commenting on anything said, still less to helping himself to one of those frosty Schaefer cans peeking suggestively through the ice cubes in the coolers under the tree. On the other hand, the Callahan men could call a gas jockey over at any time and grill him for the entertainment of the other movers—on his sex life (nonexistent, if you don't count masturbation), on how much pubic hair he had (also nonexistent for a late-blooming Celt), or on why he's working for such a maniac (Dan) in such a chickenshit job (pumping gas).

For me, these periodic grillings were just another lesson in hierarchy similar to countless others I'd been subjected to at school, church, and home. It started to creep over me that maybe pumping gas wasn't the right career for me. I'd had enough of dirty magazines, cheap talk, cigarettes, and Dan's mercurial moods. Dan was bored, and like a caged tiger pacing all day in a circle, he exhausted his active mind with irrational acts of willfulness and racist screeds to pass the time. Dan had ended up on the wrong treadmill, and he hated that. By the time I was seventeen I knew I had to get out of there. Lucky for me, for the first and only time in my life I knew exactly where I wanted to go and what I wanted to do.

I wanted, in the worst way, to exchange my light blue polyester Mobil shirt with the red Pegasus on it for the green cotton sweat-stained T-shirt festooned with the white Callahan Bros.

Moving & Storage logo and the little North American Van Lines tractor-trailer. Sweat was manhood. Sitting and drinking with the boys after work and sharing the secrets of their underworld looked like a brotherhood. My American Dream was to earn one of those shirts. I wanted the right to walk up to the tree, open a beer, casually hook the top onto the unbroken chain, and be at home and relaxed; to be in the cradle, so to speak. I wanted to be in some hierarchy where I wasn't at the bottom. Looking back on it now, I must have started out pretty low to think that being accepted as an equal by a small group of working-class drunks was a move up, but there you are. It's the truth no matter how pathetic it sounds.

———

My eighteenth birthday was May 22, 1976, and that afternoon, after school, I walked into the Callahan Bros. office, filled out an application, and was hired. When I told Dan I was going to work for Callahan, he shrugged and wished me luck. I wasn't the first or the last guy to leave Dan to go over to the movers.

On the appointed day I left my house at 7:30 a.m. for the ten-minute walk to Callahan Bros. It was humid and hot; one of those June days when the early morning temperature is hovering around eighty-five, giving you a slapping reminder of the brutal summer weather on the way. I hadn't slept much the night before because I didn't want to be late for my first day as a mover.

I arrived at Callahan's at twenty to eight, and though I was early, Bobby Rich, one of the regular guys, was already there. He said, "Hi, Murph," and looked me over as I tentatively hovered near the time clock. He asked me if I was there to service John's car, and I swelled with pride and said no, I was coming to work for Callahan's. Bobby nodded, showed me how to punch in, including how to hit the punch button before the ten-minute click so I'd be paid from 7:50 instead of 8:00, and led me downstairs to the employee room. It was a humble place permeated with the smell of cardboard boxes, which I'll take to my dying day. There was a ten-seat poker table in the corner with a Masonite cover topped with porn magazines and ashtrays. Everybody smoked. Bobby sat at the table, and when I went to sit down next to him he directed me to the sprung sofa against the wall. I may have been wearing a Callahan shirt, but I hadn't earned a place at the big table.

The guys began to trickle in, and I could hear the thump of work boots and the click of the time clock as each worker came through the door upstairs. Down they came: Little Al, the resident Mephistopheles; Ralph, the laziest drunk in southeastern Connecticut; Cuzzie, a teetotal cousin of John's from Stamford; Billy Belcher, called Bull; Richie, a huge taciturn kid they called the Gentle Giant; Jimmy, the policeman, who could drink more beer than any three men; Howard and Joe, the two black men; David, the overweight son of the boss, christened by Little Al as The Incredible Bulk; and a couple of other part-timers. All the regulars, including Howard and Joe, sat at the poker table.

In addition to me there was another new guy that day: a seven-foot two-inch colossus named Gary Rogers. I knew Gary vaguely from Little League, where he had been the home run king. When I looked at Gary I realized how little I was bringing to this moving game. I was small for my age, chicken-chested, and scared. Gary was massive and confident. He was from a posh family in Old Greenwich, and everything he'd ever done in life had been a rousing success.

TC Almy, the Callahan dispatcher, came down promptly at eight to hand out work assignments. Each assignment was on a clipboard attached to a vinyl case containing basic tools. On top was the bill of lading, which contained the vital information for the job: the address of the shipper, a listing of who was on the crew, the hourly billing rate, the destination address, and an estimate of how much time the move should take.

Moving companies like Callahan's perform four categories of moving work: local, commercial, long-distance, and international. Callahan's work was mostly local moving, which entails loading up someone's house in the morning and then unloading in the afternoon at the new house. It takes the greatest toll on the body because you are handling stuff every working day. Long-haul drivers get plenty of days when they're just sitting and driving; international moves are almost never time-sensitive, so the pace is easier; and commercial jobs—moving offices around—are mostly done with dollies and elevators. It's the local stuff that eventually kills you or drives you to drink; more commonly, both.

I was assigned that first morning to work in Little Al's crew and take part in a big commercial job moving a company from the second floor of a house in Stamford to an office building in Greenwich. The company was called International Aviation, and whatever they did required a lot of paperwork, because they had forty-five lateral file cabinets, all of them full. At a guess I'd say each one weighed 400 pounds.

We arrived at the job late because Little Al had gotten the address wrong. He had extremely poor eyesight but out of misplaced vanity he refused to wear glasses. At five feet five, with a massive beer belly and weighing over 220, he was strange-looking in an off-balance sort of way, like maybe he'd had glandular problems as a kid. He had long muttonchop sideburns, oiled hair going straight back, and a permanent wad of Copenhagen in his lip. Glasses wouldn't have made much difference to the overall impression he created, which was that of a genial circus dwarf with more than a touch of malice. Little Al's standard procedure when driving to a shipper's house was to hand the bill of lading to the guy in the shotgun seat and ask him to read off the address. This usually worked pretty well, except in this case Joe was sitting shotgun. Joe wasn't much of a reader, so when he read the street address of International Aviation, 2002 Summer Street, he told Al it was "two hundred two." Half an hour later, when we were sitting in front of the triple-decker tenement at 202 Summer Street, Little Al insisted on looking at the bill of lading. He fished out the glasses he kept for emergencies, read the number 2002, and said, "Joe, what number did you say the shipper was at?"

"Two hundred two."

"Is this the number?"

"Yup."

"You call this number two hundred two?"

"Al, don't you know nothing? Don't blame me 'cause you're blind. Two zero zero is two hundred, right?"

"Right, Joe."

"So two zero zero two is two hundred and two."

"OK, Joe. Never mind."

So we were a little late arriving. It was only eight thirty, but it was going to be a scorching hot day when everything shimmers in the distance and dogs and cats find a shady corner somewhere to wait it out. Al handed out work assignments, and, seeing as how the whole crew had known me for years as one of Dan's candy-ass gas jockeys, I was assigned to the file room. Such work I never imagined. I carried the first lateral file with Bobby Rich. Bobby was short, thick, and about fifty-five years old, and he'd been a mover his whole life

The file room was in a second-floor office, and the egress was down a winding staircase far too narrow to even consider using a hand truck. Bobby and I handled the first lateral down fairly smoothly, but there was no place to really grab the piece, and our sweaty forearms and hands made the seamless metal slippery. I couldn't believe two guys were lifting something this heavy, this bulky, this slippery, down and around a flight of stairs. I was on the bottom, of course. Bobby might have taken me under his wing, but he wasn't going to make things easy for me. Any giving way on the piece going down would have been instant death. We'd only just started, and already my arms were in agony. I was scared, and we had forty-four more laterals to bring down. I dropped the second lateral just before we got to the lip of the stairs, and the metal edge carved a crimson serpent down the inside of my forearm. *First blood*, I remember thinking, as Bobby whisked me to the men's room to stanch the bleeding. Little Al grabbed some paper towels and tried to wipe the blood off the carpet. At this, the boys took pity on me, or more likely didn't want any more blood sprayed over the shipper's office, so they assigned me to lug banker's boxes from the top of the stairs out to the truck.

My equally green colleague Gary Rogers was with me, and we commiserated together on how different this was from what we had expected. There were still forty-three more lateral files to be brought down, and my overriding thought was that they *would* be brought down. Everyone on the crew realized that this job was a bitch, but nobody ever considered not doing it. When you hired movers, they moved it. Execution was the imperative. This unequivocation was very attractive to me then, as it is now.

We finished loading at noon, piled into the truck, and drove over to Billy Graves's West End Tavern on Fairfield Avenue for lunch. The boys ate at Billy's whenever they were in Stamford because the beers were cheap, the service fast, and there was a big fenced-in parking lot in the back so John Callahan wouldn't see the truck if he happened to be driving around. It had recently become a dismissible offense to drink on the job at Callahan's. This constituted a huge break in tradition. The shift had been caused by the workers' vote to join the Teamsters Union a few months before; John Callahan felt betrayed, and since there was already language in the Teamster contract about alcohol use on the clock, John decided to enforce it verbatim. From one day to the next, anyone caught drinking would be immediately fired. This didn't change anything really. Everyone drank just as much and just as often, but now they had to hide their beers and find lunch taverns with enclosed parking lots.

In the preunion days, lunch would always be at a bar. On particularly tough jobs, John Callahan himself was known to show up late in the day with a case of beer for the crew. On road trips, it was the job of the guy in the shotgun seat to prepare a thermos of cocktails for the driver. At the end of a move, the shipper always offered us beer. Often our work would take us into New York City, which required a 7 a.m. start. At 7:20 we'd get off I-95 in Pelham and stop at Arthur's Bar and drink a couple or three screwdrivers before heading into Manhattan. As far as I could tell, the moving business floated on an ocean of alcohol.

Lunch at Billy Graves's was a frenetic affair. I had a bag of chips and kept drinking the beers that appeared in front of me. I was pretty shell-shocked by the morning's work, so I didn't really register the orgy of engorgement some of my colleagues were engaged in. It was as if someone had set a stopwatch and said, "OK, guys, you have thirty minutes, so get her done!" Jimmy ate nothing but drank at least seven beers. Richie ordered three calzones and drank four beers while waiting for them, drank two more beers while wolfing them down, and then drank two beers for dessert. Everyone else dined in a similar manner.

Someone had evidently told TC that maybe I'd better take it easy in the afternoon, because after lunch I was sent with Billy Belcher, Gary, and Ralph to work a small local job. Billy knew it was my first day and that the temperature was above ninety, so he sent me up to the attic to clean out chowder.

Now I grew up in an old Victorian house. It didn't have an attic. I'd never even seen an attic, certainly never been in one, and definitely never been in one in the middle of a hot day, after a morning of killing work, after drinking four beers at lunch on an empty stomach, and after being gently hazed by a bunch of work-worn movers, most of whom knew me as one of the skinny, hollow-chested, wiseasses from Dan's. So I didn't know there was only Sheetrock between the rafters in an attic.

I grabbed one of those plastic clothes storage hanger things to bring downstairs, stepped between the rafters, heard a crash, and opened my eyes to find myself lying on the king-size master bed one floor below clutching the clothes hanger in a tight embrace. Looking up I could see in the sheetrock the jagged outline of a human form in free fall. Billy Belcher heard the crash and came running upstairs to the attic. He couldn't find me and came down and saw me lying on the bed, fully involved with the clothes hanger, and observed: "Good thing these people are moving out and not in." Gary Rogers went up to finish the attic. Billy went to call the office.

We finished loading and stopped at the warehouse, where I cowered in the truck trying to make myself invisible. Billy Belcher came back from a brief conclave with management and told me everything was going to be OK, but I needed to relax and slow down. We then drove over to the shipper's destination house to unload. Billy told me to open the truck's side doors to get a little air into the hot truck. I went around to the side and studied the door latch for a long time. Slow down. *Relax*. I figured out the door latch and opened the side door an inch or two. I had the matter well in hand. It was only a matter of applied main force to get some air to my sweating comrades. I pulled the door a little harder and it gave a little more. *That's the ticket*, I thought, and I yanked hard. The door had given way another eight inches or so when someone yelled, "Stop!" I stopped. As is standard procedure, Billy Belcher had secured all the paintings and mirrors tightly together against the truck wall, using the strap and clip that fits into grooves along the sides. One of the clips was attached to the side door. By pulling on the door I had tightened the strap against all of the glass. By yanking on the door I had broken three mirrors, four picture frames, and the top of an antique vanity.

Billy told me to take it easy, smoke a cigarette, and fold some moving pads. Gary Rogers cleaned up the broken glass while Ralph scowled at me. Taking it easy, folding pads, and smoking cigarettes was evidently *his* job. Billy went to make another phone call.

John Callahan came out in his car to survey the damage and then drove me back to the warehouse. It was a long, quiet ride, though comfortable because John had the AC cranked up high. In fact it was the coolest I'd been all day. John was pensive and silent. We drove into the warehouse yard, and he told me to park his car and then collapse the empty moving cartons on the loading dock and put them in the dumpster. This I accomplished without incident, and frankly, I was rather proud of myself.

When four thirty rolled around and the boys began to return from their various jobs, we saw a plume of smoke rising at the far end of the yard. John Callahan's car, idling in the sun since two thirty, with the AC turned up full in the heat of a ninety-degree day, was peacefully melting down in the sunlit corner where I'd parked it two hours before. I had neglected to shut off the engine.

I wanted to run away. I never wanted to look at any of these people again, and I knew what I was going to do. I'd quit before I was fired. Bobby Rich came over, looked at me, and quietly said, "Let's go punch out, Murph." I went into the foyer where the time clock was, grabbed my virgin time card, slunk into the office, and laid it on John's desk. "I won't need this anymore. Please don't pay me for today either. I must have cost you more money today than any ten guys."

John looked up from his pile of claim forms, eyed me narrowly, paused a moment, and handed the time card back to me. "Go punch out. You'll need this card tomorrow. Don't be late, we've got a busy day."

I heard the next day that my exploits were subject number one under the tree at Dan's that afternoon. I didn't attend, needless to say, but I received the distinct impression that the general view was that I had demonstrated a lot of pluck carrying the lateral files in the morning, which showed promise, and that I was such a fuckup the boys couldn't wait to see what I'd do next and was therefore welcome.

The next morning I punched in seconds before the clock ticked ten to eight. I waited and looked for Gary Rogers, but I found out later he had called in sick.

The job was obviously too much for him.

Chapter 2
ROAD WARRIORS

After that eventful first day at Callahan's, I settled down into the rhythm of daily manual labor. I discovered that moving suited me perfectly because I could lose myself inside the work. Many young male neurotics find out early that hard labor is salve for an overactive mind. When the old guys marveled at my intensity, they were impressed. Little did they know that running up and down staircases for hours on end, carrying dressers and refrigerators and pianos, was to me a *relief* from stress. Hard work temporarily shut down the constant movie running in my brain that looped around in an endless cacophony of other people's expectations, obligation, guilt, anger, and rebellion.

My status was solid as a good worker and a good shipmate. I could be relied upon to pull my weight on the trucks, and after work, my yearning for distraction translated into an epic thirst under the tree that matched or surpassed any of the older congregants'. Work hard, drink hard. I was right there. Each day I'd punch out in my brine-streaked green T-shirt and walk over to the fence, pointedly ignoring Dan's candy-ass gas jockeys, and dig deep into the cooler for one of those frosty Schaefer cans. The truth of it was, the club wasn't all that exclusive.

———

Callahan Bros.' arch competitor in Fairfield County was Morse Moving, based in Stamford. Both companies were agents for North American Van Lines so there was occasionally some conflict as to who got credited for booking a move. Morse operated more like a bucket shop out of *Glengarry Glen Ross* than a trucking company. They had an army of aggressive salesmen and access to North American's enormous fleet. At Morse the salesmen were procuring multiple listing books, haunting mortuaries, cold-calling corporations, monitoring divorce courts, you name it. Whenever a change in personal circumstances occurred in someone's life that might conceivably trigger a relocation, there lurking in a corner would be a Morse salesman waving a binding estimate and wearing an understanding smile. Callahan Bros., on the other hand, was so well established that they sat around in the office and waited for the phone to ring, which it did, often. The cultures of Morse and Callahan were as far apart as two entities could possibly be.

Morse had a long-haul driver named Tim Wagner, a handsome white guy in his late twenties. Tim was leasing a tractor from Morse and running forty-eight states for North American when he was dispatched to load 12,000 pounds booked by Callahan's to Dallas. Tim showed up at 8 a.m. and took the trudge down the stairs to pick up his helpers. He was immediately struck by the conviviality of the crew and the relaxed authority of management. The air of entitled prosperity that permeated Callahan Bros. was a stark contrast to the hornet's nest over at Morse. At the end of the workday, having experienced Callahan's high-quality help, and further impressed with other information gleaned from the workers, Tim approached John Callahan with the idea of switching from Morse to Callahan's. Tim's proposal was to buy his own tractor and lease it to North American through Callahan Bros., who would provide the trailer and equipment. John would make less money by not owning the tractor, but he would have another truck on the road (North American was always hounding him to put on more trucks) and a great driver available when he needed one. They shook on the deal, and it wasn't more than a week later when Tim drove up in his brand-new $85,000 Peterbilt tractor looking for a trailer. All John had available was a 35-foot single-axle piece of junk from the 1950s, which clearly wasn't going to work, so John sent Tim bobtailing—driving a tractor without a trailer attached—down to Kentucky Trailer Corp., outside of Louisville, to go shopping.

Tim picked out the longest legal trailer he could, which was a beautiful 45-foot flat-floor moving van complete with belly boxes, pull-out tailgate, extra side doors, and a deck door. For the inside he bought forty steel cargo bars, six furniture dollies, four rubber dollies, two piano boards, two refrigerator dollies, two Magliner dollies, 250 large rubber bands, assorted straps and winches, fifteen sheets of plywood, a first-rate toolbox, and twenty dozen brand-new moving pads. Tim signed John's name to everything, called dispatch in Fort Wayne, and got loaded out of Madisonville, Kentucky, the next day with a full load to Seattle. John Callahan waited almost two years to see his new trailer because Tim's furious pace kept it out on the road. When Tim finally showed up in Callahan's yard, the trailer had 125,000 miles on it and was completely paid for.

One midsummer Friday afternoon about five thirty, we heard the sound of air brakes behind us in Callahan's driveway. The crew was all there under the tree, drinking beer and feeling easy and mellow. We knew that John had road drivers, but these guys weren't a part of our work life. The whole point of having road drivers was to keep them on the road. I think John liked to keep it separate for another reason, which was the equipment. An owner-operator like Tim Wagner, who was expected by the van line to go anywhere anytime, needed to be properly equipped. The road drivers had the best and latest stuff; we, the poor local movers, got the junk.

The trucks we drove were a disgrace, and the equipment was often substandard. The equipment issue was always pretty high up there in the discussion ranks under the tree, and I was a vocal critic of Callahan management about it, as was everyone else. It wasn't until much later, when I stopped to drop off something at Little Al's house, that Al took me into his garage to drink a couple of beers and showed me all the equipment he had stolen from Callahan's to outfit his moonlight moving business. Everything was stenciled PROPERTY OF CALLAHAN BROS. Al told me several other employees had similar setups, and then I became aware that the reason John wouldn't invest in equipment was that he knew it would all get stolen.

It was considered perfectly acceptable to steal from John, whether it was overtime or equipment or boozing on the clock, but I never once saw anyone steal anything from a shipper. This is not to say that we didn't open drawers or boxes, particularly if the shipper was good-looking. Then she could reasonably expect her dresser drawers to be ransacked for a look at the lingerie and sex toys. (When I started in the 1970s, it was always surprising to find a nightstand drawer with some kind of sex toy or lingerie. Nowadays it's surprising to find nothing. My advice to shippers is to either to pack your erotica yourself or salt the lingerie drawer with plastic snakes or a loaded mousetrap. This will scare and impress the movers; always a sound option.)

Anyway, it was five thirty under the tree, and there, right out of the truck wash in Milford, parked behind us in all its glory, was Tim Wagner's navy blue, chrome-hulled Peterbilt hooked to the almost-new Kentucky trailer. It was very possibly the nicest rig in the North American fleet. Tim saw us there under the tree and came over. We tried to come off as cordial but unimpressed. He turned down our offer of a beer, and someone tentatively asked if he could maybe take a look at the truck. Tim said sure, and he went around and opened the trailer and popped the lock on the passenger side of the Peterbilt. We checked out the trailer first. It was a mover's Sistine Chapel. There were rows and rows of perfectly folded, clean pads. All the equipment had a place and was stowed perfectly. The hardwood floor was polished. The trailer resembled nothing so much as an operating room scrubbed for the next surgery. Then we checked out the cab. It had a maroon velour interior with lots of gauges and lights, a large padded steering wheel, two gearshifts, and an adjustable air ride seat. The sleeper had a full-size orthopedic mattress, a seat belt, a climate control console, and a quad stereo sytem. The bed had a white goose-feather duvet, and Tim had tucked in the sheets using hospital corners. Tim's meticulous attention to order and system stood in stark relief to our own slapdash attitude toward machines and equipment. *Aha!* I said to myself. *This was how it's supposed to be done.*

When the bunch of us finished checking out the rig, Tim went into the office to drop off paperwork constituting probably another thirty grand worth of revenue, came back, and climbed up into his Pete. It started with a roar and a whine. He let the air build up, released the brakes, and pulled out of Callahan's lot with a hiss of the air dryer and a blast of the air horn.

Almost everyone under the tree had stopped drinking for a few minutes to check out Tim's truck. But not quite everyone. On the far side of the lot stood Little Al, Ralph, and Bobby, clutching their Schaefer cans, facing away from where Tim's truck had been.

John's experiment with Tim Wagner proved so successful that he was keen to sign up more drivers. John liked having prime rigs out on the road with his name all over them as much as anyone. He liked dealing with long-haul drivers who were more polished than his regular crew. John also learned that Callahan Bros. was considered a prime agent among road drivers and that he personally was considered one of the straightest guys in the business, which he was. Word got out via Tim Wagner, and soon John signed up another defector from Morse named Willie Joyce.

Willie was twenty-three, not much older than me, when I first met him. He was five feet eight inches tall and weighed about 160 pounds. He had longish brown hair, green eyes, a face pockmarked from acne, and a pointed goatee on his chin. With his quick movements and his jumpsuit, he reminded me of a very intense elf.

I had worked late and it was about 7:30 p.m. The crowd had thinned out under the tree to just Ralph and Bobby and me, but the beer cooler was full. Willie pulled in with the new trailer John had just bought for him, though he didn't have some fancy new tractor like Tim Wagner. Willie was driving an old faded blue GMC Astro 95 that didn't even have a sleeper. He called it the Cornflake.

Willie lit over the fence and asked us if anyone wanted to make twenty bucks to help him clean up the trailer. There were no introductions. Ralph and Bobby had no use for road drivers, and Willie had no use for anyone just then except someone to work. He explained that he'd finished unloading 20,000 pounds yesterday in Chicago and had driven straight back to Connecticut last night and today because he needed to load 22,000 pounds tomorrow in Greenwich bound for Florida.

I asked him what he needed, and in reply he hopped the fence again and opened the side door to the trailer. It looked like tornado wreckage. The moving pads were strewn about the floor in unfolded piles. Plywood sheets leaned against the walls in various poses of disorder. Moving equipment lay about everywhere, and on top of this mayhem, like seracs after an avalanche, were several hundred empty moving cartons of various sizes. Willie explained that he needed to get the trailer ship-shape. We started folding pads. Every driver has his way of folding pads, and Willie instructed me on his method. They had to be perfect. He stopped me a few times and quickly and impatiently showed me exactly how he wanted them done. He wasn't rude, exactly, just focused. He was direct, channeling his solid middle-class Stamford upbringing into this rough world of labor. He spoke in soft mellow tones with incredibly clear diction, and he sure sounded like a Fairfield county boy. Maybe even one who had gone to a fancy boarding school, maybe spent summers sailing on Martha's Vineyard. But Willie didn't have a filthy mouth like the preppies I knew.

While I was folding pads, Willie neatly stacked the plywood and strapped it in. Things were looking better. Then we separated by size the big rubber bands used to wrap pads around furniture and hung them on the trailer wall on hooks. Next came burlap pads, called skins, which are used for wrapping tough and dirty items like fireplace grates and garden tools. We stacked the four-wheel dollies and secured them to the wall along with the refrigerator dolly. Next, we collected the small tools lying around and put them in Willie's toolbox. Finally we swept the whole trailer from front to back. After two solid hours we'd finished and the trailer looked almost as good as Tim Wagner's.

I told Willie there was a cooler full of Schaefer's under the tree, but he said he was hungry, so we headed down the street to the Starboard Port to get some dinner. Willie ordered the chateaubriand for two, along with baked potatoes, a side of fries, a side of fried clams, and a pitcher of Heineken. I thought he was buying me dinner, but he wasn't. The ensuing rampage of consumption took him about ten minutes to finish. It looked like Willie was racing against time to get as much food and drink inside him as he could. After the last dish was taken away, Willie ordered two slices of apple pie and had his beer pitcher refilled. Then he leaned back and asked me what I was doing tomorrow. I told him I'd be working at Callahan's. He replied that he was loading a full trailer up on Stanwich Road and needed two more helpers in addition to the crew he'd already arranged. He said he'd pay me $8.50 an hour, which was $1.50 more than I made at Callahan's. If I was game he'd talk to TC in the morning.

Willie and I walked back to Callahan's yard. He opened the trailer doors, laid down some pads for a bed, and told me to be at Callahan's at 7 a.m. This guy had just worked forty-eight hours straight with an eighteen-hour day in front of him tomorrow. He'd eaten a meal no three people could have finished, drunk twelve beers, and, according to him, made over $3,000 in four days. He'd had no shower for who knows how long and was sleeping in his trailer.

I was intrigued. Tim and Willie were young guys making big money. Tim was a nobody from the wrong side of the tracks and had qualified for an $85,000 loan to buy his Peterbilt. Willie had just ordered his own new truck. In addition to that, they both had the respect and trust of a man like John Callahan, not to mention that they were willing and ready to go anywhere anytime to achieve their goals. It wasn't hard to see why guys like Ralph and Bobby chose to ignore them. The local boys were trapped, while Tim and Willie looked like revolutionaries with their flat bellies, swollen bank accounts, and attitude of complete indifference to anything but work.

The next morning, Willie was waiting for me in the Cornflake. I'd never ridden in a tractor-trailer before. All the Callahan trucks were straight trucks. I was up so high. The engine felt so powerful. This whole rig was going to be loaded today, and three days from now it would be empty in Florida. I was in.

——

The shipper's name was Lester Tabb. He had a big house in Backcountry Greenwich, where the big-money lived. We drove up and found the two pillars on the right side of the road standing guard over a long twisting driveway. Willie's helper Jeff Wilson and Jeff's sister Punky were already there. Willie tossed Jeff the trailer keys and pulled ahead. Jeff opened the side doors and pulled himself into the trailer. Willie told me to get out and block traffic. As Willie backed blind-side into the Tabb driveway, Jeff lifted the power lines with a long-handled broom. About a hundred yards down the truck stopped, and Jeff tossed out a few sheets of plywood. He jumped down and placed them over a flower bed, and Willie cut the wheel hard guiding the trailer through the twists while Jeff moved the plywood, anticipating the next move, protecting the landscaping, and keeping the drive wheels out of the mud. The two of them were doing a dance they'd clearly done before.

After half an hour of this, the mansion hove into view. It was an ivy-covered faux Tudor pile from the 1920s, three stories with steep gables and a slate roof. I expected to see gargoyles leering over the gutters. Willie backed right to the front door, and we dropped the walkboard into the foyer.

Looking around, I realized we had a twenty-five-room mansion to empty. I figured we'd be here several days. The first item to be loaded was a Persian carpet forty feet wide and sixty feet long. All rolled up it was about four feet high, and the five of us tried to lift it. Not a chance. We could barely pick up one end. Jeff ran back into the truck—he always ran when he worked—and returned with four four-wheel dollies. As we lifted up each section of the rug, Punky slid a dolly underneath. In no time the rug was atop the four dollies, and it looked like a mutated python from a 1950s horror movie. With Punky steering, we rolled the rug through the drawing room and up the walkboard into the trailer. Jeff had set up ropes at intervals, and we pushed the rug to the front of the trailer. We put the ropes around the rug and lifted it in sections, with Punky pulling the rope tight as it went toward the trailer's roof. It was now well past 9 a.m. Willie told me to go down to the cellar and clean out chowder.

By noon I had carried everything from the basement and set it outside the truck. All the truck doors were open, and Willie could see everything, so he worked my chowder into holes in his tiers as he loaded. He was in his loading trance. He had a picture in his mind of every item in the house and was visualizing the location of the next piece in the tier. He and Jeff had been working together for years, and Jeff was prescient about what Willie would want next.

When we stopped for lunch, we all sat down inside the trailer in the shade. (Movers never eat in the shipper's house.) I had brought a peanut butter sandwich, two Oreos, and a bottle of Gatorade. Jeff brought his cooler into the truck and undid the clasp. The thing popped open like a jack-in-the-box. Jeff pulled out two loaves of Wonder Bread and what appeared to be the entire contents of an Italian deli: ham, salami, roast beef, tuna, egg salad, macaroni salad, four kinds of cheese, French's mustard, Dijon mustard, horseradish, mayonnaise, potato salad, napkins, cutlery, a couple of 64-ounce bottles of Coke, a couple of bottles of Gatorade, and an entire cherry pie. In a bag next to the cooler were the dry goods: a jumbo bag of Doritos, a jar of peanut butter, a jar of Bonne Maman jelly, two boxes of Fig Newtons, and a banana. While I morosely munched my sandwich and eyed Jeff's larder, Willie, still in his loading trance, stared remotely into the distance, no doubt building the after-lunch tier in his head. Willie also knew there was no way we were going to get everything into this trailer and we'd have to leave some things behind. It's called an overflow. Mr. Tabb would not like that, and John Callahan wouldn't either, so Willie was trying to figure out when to break the bad news. Finally, he was figuring how to maximize the weight of the load, because he's paid by weight. Whoever was going to take the overflow might as well take the thin metal shelving, the clothing cartons, and all the other light, bulky stuff. Willie would take the file cabinets, book cartons, refrigerators, dressers, gun safe, and dumbbells. On the other hand, Mr. Tabb would go crazy if the overflow took a week or so to get there, leaving him with no clothes. It was a tricky problem, and Willie wandered around during the fifteen minutes he allowed for lunch, idly nibbling a Fig Newton. Jeff, meanwhile, had built himself a four-decker Dagwood using half the first loaf of Wonder Bread. It was disgusting. Jeff was gorging himself like Jabba the Hutt, shoving whatever he could get into his mouth and spilling the Coke down his front. This was the second time in less than eighteen hours I'd seen someone eat like that.

When lunch was over, Willie informed us that since we'd had such an easy morning there would be no breaks the rest of the day. He told Jeff to empty the library, so Jeff brought out his prized humpstrap. (A humpstrap is a hemp mesh strap about three inches wide and ten feet long, which can be used to efficiently move large items. It is particularly useful for negotiating a bureau or dresser down a twisted set of stairs and for carrying multiple cartons.) In the library, Jeff laid his humpstrap on the floor, stacked five book cartons on it, and then laid a second row of five. He picked up the strap, twisted it tight against his chest, leaned over, transferring the weight onto his back, and carried ten book cartons (about 500 pounds) down two flights of stairs into the truck. Jeff is an animal. Willie had the gleam in his eye once he'd seen Jeff bring down over 7,000 pounds of books. If Willie could smile while he was working, he'd have smiled then.

All of us were in that sweet spot now that we'd established the rhythm. Willie built his tiers: dresser, piano, nightstands, end tables, dining room chairs, chowder. Next tier: washer, dryer, overstuffed furniture, chowder. Next tier: tool bench, cartons, chowder. We worked nine hours after lunch nonstop. By 9 p.m. the pile of chowder in the driveway was gone, and there was room for one more tier. Jeff brought out a row of six fireproof file cabinets. At 9:45 Willie closed the trailer doors; we were full. I was fried to a crisp and sat on the grass to light up a smoke. Jeff was on a ladder attaching straps to the slots on the outside of the trailer. Willie looked at me like I'd gone crazy and told me to get the rest of the file cabinets from the office.

"What for?" I asked. "There's no more room."

"Get them."

Willie pulled out the tailgate, a steel platform hidden under the rear bumper, while I went inside and wheeled out the six file cabinets. He set them up on the tailgate and stacked a lawn mower, a picnic table, and the ladder on top. Another 1,500 pounds. Jeff covered the load with a tarp and strapped it all in using the side clips. It was 10:15.

Mr. Tabb was unhappy about the overflow, but he was too exhausted to care very much. Willie had waited until the end to tell him for that very reason. I was exhausted too. I climbed into the cab and tried to arrange a place to sit. The seat area was taken up with Willie's toolbox, moving pads, and a four-wheel dolly that wouldn't fit in the trailer. I perched there for the twenty-minute ride back to Callahan's. I found out later that the shipment weighed 25,750 pounds. Willie netted almost five grand on the Tabb move, bringing his eight-day net to a shade less than $8,000. Callahan Bros. made way more than that. I made $140 on a day when I would have normally made $56. Walking home after Willie dropped me off, I was in an endorphin-induced euphoria. Yes, I was completely exhausted, but I was exultant too. I had been a key member of a professional team with a fixed and difficult objective. Nobody had wasted a word or a motion through sixteen hours of totally focused *execution*. Give me more of that! I collapsed into bed happier than I'd been for as long as I could remember.

From then on I was Willie's lumper whenever he came to Connecticut. I even got a road trip out of it when he had to do a quick turn to Virginia Beach. He was traveling at that point with Diana, a preppie chick with a perfect figure, fine features, and a bubbly personality. For an ugly guy, Willie had a way with women. I never did understand it and still don't. Diana had been trained for voice. She had a playful "come to bed with me" singing voice like Joey Heatherton. I'll always remember traveling Route 17 south toward Virginia Beach crossing the Chesapeake Bay Bridge-Tunnel for the first time, at sunset, with Diana sitting cross-legged in the sleeper singing sixteenth-century madrigals. Willie told me that Diana had suggested early on that every time they crossed a new state line they should pull over and screw and see how many states they could cover. Diana rode the road with Willie for almost a year before they called it off. By the time she left they had notched off forty-six states.

———

Over the next year or two I worked with Willie once in a while, but since he was running the coasts he was gone for months at a time. In any case, moving had become a secondary consideration. In the fall of 1977 I entered Colby College.

This isn't the appropriate forum for a disquisition on how I squandered my college opportunities. The CliffsNotes version is that I spent three years in Waterville, Maine, smoking as much dope and expending as little effort on my studies as I could. The reason for this, I know now, was that I had already been seduced. Dan Bartoli and Callahan Bros. had begun the fraying of my umbilical cord of blue blazers, church, junior golf, and suburban upward mobility. Encountering Willie Joyce severed it completely. I'd begun my working career at the very bottom of the employment heap at Dan's. Having started there, I decided I'd pull myself up the economic ladder by determination and work. I'd show the boys under the tree it wasn't the system that kept them down, and I'd show my teachers and my parents that college wasn't necessary to achieve success. To put it another way: Screw you, everybody. The American Dream is alive and well. From now on I'll be the captain of my ship and the master of my soul.

Colby had an independent study scheme they called the January Plan. The concept of the Jan Plan, as it was known, was to provide an opportunity for students to pursue independent study projects off-site during the long break between Christmas and mid-February. (Cynics remarked that the Jan Plan also allowed the school to save lots of money by not heating dorms through the shank of a Central Maine winter.) Any project would do so long as you could find a faculty member to sign off on it. My first Jan Plan consisted of a month at a Virginia commune modeled on the book *Walden Two* by B. F. Skinner. The brief time I spent there permanently cured my nascent penchant for collectivism. I skipped the Jan Plan during my sophomore year like I skipped a lot of things. My junior year Jan Plan was decidedly less idealistic. Since I was flat broke, I figured I could work for Willie and write up the economics of long-haul movers as my Jan Plan. All I had to do was find a professor to sign off on the idea. I found a professor in the Economics Department who thought it was an OK idea; he wasn't thrilled about it, but he was packing his office in preparation for his own Jan Plan in Baja, so he signed it off.

I called TC at Callahan Bros. and asked him to have Willie Joyce call me when he next checked in. Willie called a few days later and said he'd pick me up at the Indianapolis airport. He'd pay me $250 a week and cover my food and lodging.

My sister Byrne drove me to Kennedy Airport on Christmas night 1979. I had a duffle bag stuffed with North American shirts, my fleece lined North American jacket, and some notebooks. I exited the terminal in Indianapolis at midnight and just about bumped into Willie's rig. He'd gotten rid of the Cornflake and purchased a brand-new Astro 95 complete with blue North American trim, oversize fuel tanks, a Cummins 290 diesel engine, and, best of all, a sleeper. Finally, he had a tractor to match his gleaming trailer.

Willie was in the forty-eight-state fleet for North American. Long-haul moving in the winter is more difficult. There's less coast-to-coast work and many more smaller, short-haul moves. It's a challenge because short-haul point-to-point moving can keep a driver away from home even longer than usual. And, there's more actual work; the more short-hauls you do, the more loading and unloading, which means more labor to hire. This exacerbates the most intractable problem a driver encounters on the road, which is finding good help. It's expensive to keep a helper with you all the time and can also become annoying. You're with this person constantly, and if the chemistry's wrong, things can get ugly fast. My call to Willie answered his own dilemma perfectly. We had worked together previously so we knew each other's habits, and Willie wanted someone he could work with through the worst part of the winter, but he didn't want a permanent person on his payroll.

We went everywhere in those six weeks. I had my first huevos rancheros in Laredo, Texas; stepped on the ice of a frozen Lake Superior in Duluth; bailed Willie out of jail in Davenport, Iowa; drove through Holcomb, Kansas—the scene of the murders that Truman Capote had memorialized in *In Cold Blood*—on a spooky, snowy night; drank my first Coors in Durango and ate a buffalo steak at the Buckhorn Exchange in Denver. We drove across the White Sands Missile Range in New Mexico (we were moving the commanding officer), played the slots in Vegas, descended Grapevine into Los Angeles, ate jambalaya in Baton Rouge, and nearly jackknifed the truck on black ice outside of Flagstaff; I dipped my toes in the Pacific Ocean underneath the Santa Monica Pier. I learned firsthand about life in the truckstops and how movers were treated as pariahs. I learned about the van line/agent system and listened to other movers talk about loads, revenue, and tricks of the trade. It was a deep immersion into the intricacies of long-haul moving, and I loved every minute of it.

I returned to Colby in mid-February 1980 with $1,500 in my pocket and the conviction that, however silly it sounded to other people, I liked meeting and getting to know the people we moved and I liked the physical labor. Driving a lot of miles wasn't so great, nor was truckstop living, but the rewards of the work, and the money, made up for a lot. The last thing I brought home with me was the certain knowledge that a long-haul mover made a minimum of $2,000 a week and sometimes much more. I couldn't put that thought away. I went back to college, studied reasonably hard, but more or less continued my idiotic life there. Something had to change, and the form of that change was beginning to coalesce into a plan. Certain people were not going to like my plan.

My stint with Willie had cleaned up my financial difficulties, and my Jan Plan on the economics of long-haul truckers received a passing grade. Whatever else it said, that report contained a nugget of truth: A young man with no prospects, no connections, and no money could launch himself by becoming a driver for a van line. For Willie, work was an enforced savings plan, which would finance his future acquisition of the entire moving industry. Willie was a renegade with a hot temper, and he knew he'd never make it in the traditional workforce. I too had decided, for similar reasons, that I'd be self-employed for life and I'd need a nest egg. Most important of all, becoming a long-haul driver would free me from the callow existence I had fashioned at Colby College.

My parents came up to Maine that May to bring some of my stuff down to Connecticut for the summer vacation. I hosted a cocktail party and invited a group of friends and professors to meet them. My father, who had never attended college and therefore had rigid ideas as to what college life should be like, heartily approved. I can see him standing next to the little bar setup I'd made (I even hired a bartender for the occasion, thanks to my flush bank account), chatting amiably with our East German exchange professor. My father stood there smoking his pipe and sipping his scotch, no doubt thinking that an informal exchange of ideas with a real Communist over Johnnie Walker fit perfectly within his fixed ideal of a liberal arts college social. He and my mother schmoozed the profs and my friends. I wanted them to have a particularly good time because very soon we were going to have the big talk.

The next morning, after croquet and mimosas on the quad, I suggested to my parents we take a stroll. The three of us walked around the campus and I finally introduced the topic that had been on my mind since returning to Maine from my road trip with Willie.

"I've got some good news and some bad news."

"What's that?" asked my father.

"Well, the good news is I've got a high-paying job working for myself where I can put some money away for whatever future I might have. The bad news is that I'm not planning to come back here and finish my degree."

"Surely this job, whatever it is," said my father, "will be available a year from now. We've seen what you've done here; you have nice friends and seem to have established some friendships with your professors. Your grades have really improved, and, well, you seem to have built quite a comfortable life here."

"Well, that's right. In a way it's too comfortable."

"What does that mean?"

"It means I'm ready to get on with things. You're seeing the best of what goes on here. You're not seeing, and I don't want you to see, the other side. I'm wasting a lot of time and a lot of your money, and I think I've taken everything this place can offer me."

"Well, one thing this place can offer you is a college degree, if you finish."

"Yes, that's true. If I finish. The thing is . . . another year here might finish me first."

"In what way?"

"Well, you saw the bar setup, you saw my long-haired friends.

I didn't want to get into this, but I'm smoking a lot of pot. In addition to that, my professors are leaving, my friends are all graduating . . . If I stay here, it's going to be miserable."

"It's only another year. It will go by so fast," my mother chimed in.

"To you maybe it will. To me it won't."

"What's this job you mentioned?" My father changed the subject.

"Well, I talked to John Callahan, and he told me he had a truck available. He said when I come home later this month he'll have one of the guys teach me how to drive it. After some practice I'll take the tractor-trailer test and get my commercial driver's license. John told me that North American is desperate for drivers, so he'll lease me the truck and contract me to North American into their long-haul fleet. I'll be making almost a hundred grand a year."

There was a long pause while we all pretended to take in the vista of the forest blanketing the hills of Central Maine.

"You want to become a truck driver?"

"Well, yes. For now."

"And you want to quit college after you've completed three years . . . to become a *truck driver*?"

"That's right."

"I think you should finish your degree," my father snapped. "After that you can do whatever you want."

"Actually," I said evenly, "I can do whatever I want right now."

"Not under my roof you can't."

"Jack," cut in my mother, "Jack, let's talk about this later." My mother had come in as peacemaker, and my father wanted to escalate. This was opposite their traditional roles.

They went off back to the motel in town. I was relatively sanguine. Things might have gone much worse.

They put my stuff in their car and returned to Connecticut. We never did talk about it in any real way ever again.

———

I finished my junior year with the best grades I'd ever gotten and moved into the basement at the family house in Cos Cob. I spent the early summer working local for Callahan's. After work, instead of drinking beer under the tree, I'd hook up the old International Harvester tractor to a 35-foot trailer and head up to St. Catherine's parking lot. There I'd set out traffic cones and practice backing up the trailer, parking, and shifting gears. I got my CDL in late June of 1980, and on July 2, I called up my first dispatcher and got my first move: 22,000 pounds, a full load, from Mount Holly, New Jersey, to Asheville, North Carolina. I went home and told my parents I'd be hitting the road the next morning. That night my father came down to the basement. In his hand he had some papers.

"Since you appear to be set on this course of action, an action which you are aware I strongly disagree with, I thought we might finalize some financial arrangements."

"Sure," I said.

"This first page is the tuition we've paid to Colby for the past three years, which we'd like you to pay back. The next page is the rent you owe us for the past three summers. The third page is the rent you'll pay if you want to continue occupying these premises."

I stared at him in disbelief. Then my incredulity turned to anger. I shouted at him, "You fucking asshole!"

"Don't use that language in my house."

"I won't use anything in your goddamn house."

I packed up my clothes and went down to Callahan's. At least I'd have free storage.

That night I slept in the sleeper of the gleaming new Astro 95 that John Callahan had just bought for me. I was up early and crossed the George Washington Bridge in the dawn's early light. I could just make out the profile of the Tappan Zee Bridge upriver. Bridges, ha! It'd been a rough few months of bridges, crossing some and burning some, but everything had been reduced to simplicity. I was free.

My parents and I didn't speak for two years.

I was a long-haul trucker now.

Chapter 3
TENDERFOOT

The first rule of truck driving is: Don't let anyone ever tell you what to do with your truck. I failed my first test of this precept early on and never failed again.

I was only about four months into the job with North American and still pretty green when I moved a guy named Mel King from Greenwich to Richmond, Virginia. Mr. King was some kind of big executive and conceived an instant dislike for me. The loading part in Greenwich went smoothly, mostly because I had hired Callahan's local crew for helpers.

It was at destination where things began to unravel. I had arrived at Mr. King's on schedule with two helpers from the local agent and a full truck loaded with his stuff. Mr. King's dream house had one of those long, curving driveways that the Richmond exurbs sprout like anthrax spores. I haven't any good reason to explain it but I cannot stand Richmond. I call the whole area a hotbed of social rest. The term is not original with me but it works. It probably has something to do with a string of problem shippers but I don't know. I surveyed the driveway and decided that even if I could get the truck down to the house, which I didn't think I could, I'd never get it out. Strictly speaking, basic physics dictates that any object in one place can extricate itself by exactly reversing the movements it took to get there. While this is theoretically true, try explaining that to a lobster caught in a trap or to a trucker pulling a trailer through a half-mile curving driveway. First rule for the lobster and the trucker ought to be: *Back in.*

I told Mr. King I didn't think I could get the truck to the house and we'd have to do a shuttle. (A shuttle is when you transfer the goods from the big truck to a smaller one.) Mr. King didn't like this idea at all, so when I called Callahan's to tell them about the shuttle, Mr. King grabbed the phone from me and complained to TC that he wasn't going to pay any shuttle charges because it was Callahan's fault for sending a driver who wasn't competent enough to operate the vehicle through a few twists and turns. Mr. King didn't care about the shuttle charges; it was a company move, after all. He was just using it as an angle to humiliate me.

Naturally, that pissed me off. Partly because he was right, in the sense that I wasn't totally competent in the job, and partly because Mr. King had taken every opportunity to belittle me from the moment we'd met. He was annoyed, I think, because as a corporate big shot he thought he should have gotten the best, most experienced driver in the North American fleet. Instead he got me. In consequence of all this, I got back on the phone and told TC I'd do my best and told Mr. King I'd try to get the truck down the driveway. One of my helpers that day was an elderly black man who called himself Frog. (Movers who work for road drivers always have their own handles to keep the tax man at a distance.) He was an old moving pro who carried his own tool pouch and lunch pail. Frog took one languid look at the driveway and drawled under his breath, "Don't do it, Junior. They'll be using that trailer to plant geraniums, 'cause that trailer ain't coming out if it ever goes in."

Frog was going way out of his way to help me. He knew, as a black man from Richmond, that you let white people do what white people are going to do. At the same time, he saw my inexperience and the weird dynamic between Mr. King and me and probably figured that my being a young fool trumped my color, so he piped up with his sage counsel.

Casting aside all advice, I started up the rig and drove down the slope toward the first bend. That one I negotiated fine, though I had to get really close to the trees on the right so that the back left wheels of the trailer would clear the trees on the other side. Now there would be no going back. The next turn was a dogleg right, and my tractor wheels started spinning because of the sharp angle, the grade, and the red clay soil I was digging up. I made that just fine too. The third turn was another dogleg right, and I took all the room to the left that I had as early as possible, but there just wasn't enough room. There was a tree in front of me and a tree within the angle of the trailer wheels. The tree within the angle was small so I shifted into my lowest gear and gunned it, figuring I'd just knock it over. Instead, the steel side of the trailer buckled against it and I was firmly wedged. Stuck. Really stuck. There was no chance of a shuttle now. In fact, emptying the truck and moving in Mr. King's family became a consideration secondary to extricating Mr. Callahan's $100,000 rig from the surrounding flora.

I turned off the engine. Silence. Calm. I got down from the truck, lit a cigarette, surveyed the situation, and started pondering options. Just then Mr. King ran up to me, his face purple with rage.

"You stupid little fuck! What are you gonna do now? My family's in there waiting to move in!" His spittle was spraying in my face.

I looked at Mr. King. I knew now how his rants and insults had magnified my insecurity and self-doubt, plunging us both into an inexorable cataract of bad judgment and ill-conceived actions. I grew up a lot in the next minute or so. I realized that his need to bully and my need to prove myself had mixed this incendiary cocktail. I wasn't ever going to play that game again. I was cured. I looked down at Mr. King, flicked my cigarette into the woods, and said, "I've got to see about getting this rig back onto some pavement. Where's your phone?"

We trudged down to his new house, past the pale, wriggling shadows of his wife and daughters, into the empty study. I combed the Yellow Pages for the biggest, baddest tow truck in Richmond. I found one, and it arrived about an hour later. The driver, John Amos, was a muscled African American about thirty years old, highly skilled in his job, and so inured to the ways of truckers that he conveyed nothing when he saw my truck corkscrewed into the woods between two trees. I respected his degree of self-control, since he couldn't have seen anything like it in all of his years towing big trucks. It must have taken all he had not to burst out laughing. I can see him back at the garage at the end of the day regaling his fellows about the Yankee truck with the child driver who had poured his rig down a drain and pulled the cork in after him.

John Amos set up the tow truck on a level spot at the top of the driveway and unleashed a fat cable with a hook on one end and a very large winch on the other. He hooked the cable to my trailer axle and started the winch to pull the trailer out. We couldn't get a straight pull, so we snaked the cable around a small tree to get the proper angle. Turning on the winch, the cable sliced through the tree with a puff of smoke and a sharp twang. The tree came down, further blocking our way.

Plan B was to position the tow truck closer to the trailer with a straighter shot and remove a couple of smaller trees. John Amos, of course, had a chainsaw in the bed of his tow truck. At the sound of the saw, Mr. King reappeared to demand what the fuck I was doing cutting down his forest, pontificating that he'd bought this house because of the woods, that I would pay for every goddamn tree I cut down, and that he was going to go back to the house this instant and call the local agent to send the insurance adjuster because he was going to file the biggest claim ever filed against the damn van line for fucking up his forest. I noticed he directed all of this at me, ignoring the towering John Amos. Had Mr. King confronted him directly, the situation might have become more complicated. John Amos could have cut the bastard in half with or without the chainsaw, but he knew the odds to the decimal point how that would pan out in Richmond.

"I'm gonna own this fuckin' van line when we're done, you little bastard" was Mr. King's parting shot.

John Amos's plan worked, and between me putting the tractor in reverse, easing the load on the winch, and John Amos constantly repositioning the tow truck to correct for the proper angle, we eased out of the woods a few inches at a time. Six hours later we had the truck on safe pavement, and we only had to cut down nine more trees. John Amos took off, having collected a cool $1,600, and it was 4 p.m. The insurance adjuster had arrived and was waiting inside Mr. King's house to interview me. I had to be in Fredericksburg the next morning at 8 with an empty truck to load a new shipment to Missouri.

The interview went quickly. The insurance guy was sitting on the floor of an empty bedroom with a notebook and pocket tape recorder. Mr. King was standing, looking out the window. I entered the room. The adjuster turned on the tape recorder.

"Mr. Murphy, can you please describe the events that occurred today, resulting in the loss of twelve trees on this property?"

"Yes sir. Earlier this morning, in attempting to unload at the King residence, I went too far down the driveway with my truck and got it stuck. In order to extract the truck, the tow truck operator was required to cut down several trees."

Mr. King butted in. "Did you verify it's twelve fucking trees? A dozen beautiful fucking hardwoods?"

"Mr. Murphy, do you dispute the number of trees?"

"No, sir."

Mr. King kicked in again. "Hardwoods, goddammit. Hardwoods, all of 'em."

"Mr. King, I'm going to have to ask you to leave the room." He headed for the door, muttering, *"Hardwoods,"* all the way down the stairs.

"Mr. Murphy, were all of the trees cut down hardwoods?"

"I can't say, sir. I don't know my trees. All I can say is that all of the trees cut down were in the way. Can I ask you a question?"

"Sure, Mr. Murphy, ask away."

"Is this going to be some massive claim?"

The insurance adjuster reached over and turned off the RECORD button. "Mel downstairs thinks he's going to get a check for what it would cost to get every tree replaced and replanted by the guys at the garden center. So suppose you go out and buy a twenty-five-year-old oak tree and move it in with a big tree mover and plant it where the old one was. That's probably five grand. Multiply that by twelve trees, and old Mel here has probably already spent the sixty grand on a tricked-out bass boat. But here's the deal: Loss of trees in a situation like this is calculated as a percentage of trees lost as a percentage of the land's value. This here's a five-acre lot worth about a hundred grand. The value of the trees is a tenth of that, so say ten grand worth of trees. There are a thousand trees on this lot, and you killed twelve of them. so that's .012 percent of ten grand. Mel's got $120 coming."

"Why are you telling me this?"

"Two reasons. One is we're on the same side. The van line is my client. The other is Mel's an asshole. I could smell him a mile off. And you look like you've had a pretty bad day."

"Thanks. My day's not even close to being over yet."

"Fuck Mel. You take care of yourself."

I still needed to get the truck unloaded. It was a job that would take three experienced men about six hours under normal conditions. It was four thirty, and the truck was half a mile from the house. *Screw it*, I thought. Drastic times called for drastic measures: I called the local Manpower office and asked for twelve movers for immediate work going until midnight. Amazingly, they said there would be a van full of men with me in less than an hour.

I went back to the truck and prepared to unload. I opened the back doors, set up the walkboard, and instructed my two helpers about what was about to happen. I'd been paying them for dozing and smoking and wandering around since this morning. Frog never said another word to me after his initial advice. Mr. King picked this time to come back and tell me that his whole family was tired, that it was almost 5 p.m., and that we should pick up tomorrow at 8 a.m. sharp.

"Sorry, Mr. King. We're unloading now. We'll be done today, or tonight, rather."

"Three of you walking a half mile? No fucking way. It will take you three days."

Just then the Manpower van pulled up, and a dozen workers of various types spilled out onto the pavement. Some of them looked a little worse for wear. Mr. King decided not to argue and scurried homeward to defend his womenfolk against this armada. Laborers who are available at a moment's notice for any kind of work that might take all night are generally people who have run out of traditional options. Mr. King had probably never seen this end of the American employment pool. His American Dream doesn't take note of economic losers, so he, and others like him, tend to treat such people as invisible—until a couple of them are carrying your sacred marriage bed into the master bedroom suite with the Jack and Jill closets, separate toilets, and the Jacuzzi tub.

My crew was reasonably diligent, and we emptied the truck by eleven thirty. We were just finishing up the last loose ends, putting beds together and bolting legs onto tables, when I realized I didn't have any money to pay the crew. I had left Connecticut the day before with $2,000 to cover labor, fuel, and lodging, which would normally last over a week. But the tow truck had taken $1,600 and I had a labor bill of two men for fifteen hours and twelve additional men for eight hours, for a total of more than a thousand dollars. In my pocket I had $175.

Temporary employment offices like Manpower operate on a cost-plus basis. They charge a certain rate per hour per person, and they pay the person a certain portion of that hourly rate and keep the rest for taxes, overhead, and profit. The Manpower people had given the work invoice to one of the men, and I was instructed to pay the crew the rate on the invoice; Manpower would bill Callahan for the rest, and Callahan would then debit my account. This wasn't how Manpower usually worked, but nobody from the local office was going to be around at midnight to distribute wages, and it's not like the guys in my crew could wait a day to pick up their pay. These folks needed to get paid so they could eat.

I was in a quandary. I was too young to have a credit card. A personal check would have been a cruel joke, since none of my workers would have bank accounts. In the end I called up TC just before midnight and asked him to wire me $2,000 via Western Union. TC wasn't too pleased about being called at home in the middle of the night, but he wasn't too miffed either. He knew I'd had a bad day because Mr. King had called him several times complaining about what a fucked-up move he'd gotten. TC never minded too much when a driver called late at night with a money request because, as he told me once, he was going to be back in bed in less than five minutes, whereas we were still dealing with the flat tire or the accident report or the freezing cold or the blazing heat or the tow truck or, in my case, the help.

I told the crew I had to drive to the truckstop in Doswell, north of Richmond, to pick up the cash to pay them. This was about thirty minutes away, and they grumbled a lot. I told them they'd all be paid for an extra hour and I'd add in taxi fare for everyone to get home. That settled them down. I put five of them in the tractor, four in the sleeper and one in the passenger seat, and put the other nine in the trailer. You see this often with straight trucks where a crew is inside the van with the door strapped open, but you don't see it often with a trailer.

At the truckstop, I stopped at the fuel island and let everyone out. In the dark, it must have looked like a Rio Grande coyote was unloading a shipment of border crossers. I bought some fuel, and they cashed my Western Union check, thank heaven, and I paid everyone off. For the first time in months I splurged and rented a motel room. This trip was a total bust. My labor bill at destination should have been about a hundred dollars; instead it was over a thousand. I'd paid the tow truck bill, plus there was body damage to the trailer that I'd have to have fixed before I brought the truck back. You can't swipe a tree aside, even a small one, with the side of a trailer. I knew that now. I crawled into bed at half past midnight and set the alarm for 5:30 a.m. I'd left this same truckstop exactly eighteen hours earlier.

Just before falling asleep, I thought through the day: I had lost money on the job, the shipper was *extremely* dissatisfied, and the management at Callahan Bros. were probably reviewing their options with respect to my contract. But the more I thought about it, the more I realized that from the moment my truck was wedged between the trees and I put Mr. King out of my mind, my judgment and actions had improved. It was my first big lesson in aggressive problem solving. Nobody was going to help me. No excuses would improve the situation, and there would be nobody around to blame or lean on. I don't think I had ever before been thrown completely onto my own resources without a backstop. Lying in that motel room I started to giggle, realizing in that wonderful moment that I'd been a mewling child my whole life. Getting stuck in the trees in order to prove my skills to Mr. King and TC and even Frog had certainly proved everything about my skills. I had none. As I thought about it even more, my giggle turned to a laugh. When I turned off the truck in the woods and climbed down to meet Mr. King, my destiny was balanced on a knife edge. I could continue the way I had been or I could change. It could have gone either way, but something smart within me decided to leave the man-child behind. It was by no means a conscious decision. When I flicked my smoke into the woods and took a good look at Mr. King, I was no longer a scared kid. I got the truck out, found the labor I needed, emptied the truck, and paid the help. Goddamn! It was funny and energizing to know that I was leaving a lot of things behind, but it was also terrifying to understand that I was now committed. The King saga was the beginning of my life as a real long-haul driver.

I had a long way to go, but I'd started.

PART II
THE
POWERLANE

Chapter 4
HAMMER DOWN

"Driver Murphy, 6518. Howzitgoin, good? Good. I've got news."

It was Gary Greene, my longtime dispatcher at North American Van Lines in Fort Wayne, Indiana. I was shooting a game of pool at the Boot Hill Saloon in Daytona and waiting for a load north when he called. It was my ninth year as a driver and I was a grizzled veteran. North American had assigned me to the Florida Powerlane, which was the coveted run from the Northeast down to Florida. The Powerlane was reserved for furious and frenzied drivers like me who could turn loads fast. The beauty of the Powerlane was that I'd always go down with a full load; the ugly part was that because so many more people moved *to* Florida than *from* Florida, it was always difficult to get a full load, or any load, coming out.

"Stop fuckin' around, Gary. Whaddya got?" Gary talked to road drivers all day long. He was completely impervious to bad attitudes or impatience. Besides, we'd been working together for years. We were like an old married couple except I was looking to do some stepping out. Not with a new dispatcher, but a new life. I

was almost thirty, had some money put away, and the years on the
road had made my world very small.

"The good news is I got you a full load. The bad news is that
you're loading in Vermont, someplace called St. Johnsbury, which
I think actually is in the United States, though barely. You're loading Monday morning, and according to the tariff book it's only
1,688 miles from Daytona. Since today is Friday I know you can
get there in plenty of time. Ready? OK, listen up." Then he gave
me my load particulars in the quick deadpan of a horse race
announcer:

9/21AM OA Woodway St. Johnsbury Shipper Murray 1,000 SIT
line haul $1,500 DA Kendall

9/21AM OA Woodway Shipper Howell 1,000 res line haul
$1,600 DA Accredited Largo

9/21PM OA McClure Essex Junction Shipper Gross 2,200 SIT
line haul $1,800 DA Atlantic Sarasota

9/21PM OA McClure Essex Junction Shipper Warren 1,200 SIT
line haul $1,600 DA Murray Fort Lauderdale

9/22AM OA CMS Bangor Shipper Taylor 3,000 res line haul
$2,400 DA Ray Naples

9/23AM OA Ray Manchester Shipper Fowler 4,000 res line
haul $4,200 DA Accredited Largo

9/24 OA Stewart Liner Newburgh Shipper McNab 8,000 res
line haul $6,000 DA A1 Key West

"Got it?" he finished.

"Got it."

"Go get 'em, kid. No claims this trip, right?"

"Right. See ya, Gary. Gotta get rolling."

Here's the translation: 9/21AM meant September 21 in the

morning. OA was the origin agent who booked the move. That's where I'd pick up paperwork and arrange for helpers. I had a directory in my truck that listed all the North American agents, so Gary kept it all in shorthand. Murray was the shipper, and 1,000 pounds the estimated weight of the shipment. SIT (storage in transit) meant I'd be loading out of Woodway's warehouse and not out of a residence, which is represented as "res." Line haul was what the shipment would pay, and DA was the destination agent, which told me where the shipment was going.

I was figuring out a bunch of things all at once; what I had here was 20,400 pounds, loading in seven shipments on four different days. It had a line haul of $19,200, which was solid, but I don't get a paid a nickel to drive empty, called deadheading, up to Vermont. That would cost me $1,000 in fuel and tolls, plus marginal expenses in cigarettes and Dr Colas (half Dr Pepper and half Coca-Cola, loaded to the brim with ice—my trademark road-sprint drink). I would start back south on the 23rd and unload Beverly Hills, Largo, and Sarasota on the 25th, unload Naples, Fort Lauderdale, and Kendall on the 26th, and finish in Key West on Sunday the 27th. The categorical imperative would be for me to be empty and ready to load on Monday the 28th. Movers are busiest at month end, when house closings occur and lease periods end. All I can do is set up my schedule to be ready at the right time. Full loads out of Florida were so rare that Powerlane drivers called one a "Pot of Gold."

———

I woke the next morning at five thirty and headed north. I had 1,700 miles to do in forty-eight hours. (That's the same as going from Philadelphia to Denver.) I needed to keep the hammer down and break the back of the trip on day one. I generally enjoy a couple of days driving because it's easy. I don't have to worry about getting help, lifting stuff, or dealing with shippers, but this was a marathon, not to mention highly illegal since I'm only allowed to drive ten hours per day.

I filled up with fuel at the Ormond Beach truckstop for $800, checked my fluids, restarted my logbook, cleaned my windshields inside and out, examined the wipers, grabbed a couple of extra gallons of Rotella motor oil, and remade the bed in my sleeper. Then I changed into a loose shirt, shorts, and sneakers, bought two Dr Colas, three packs of smokes, and an audiobook. I was ready for the northbound dash and my truck was too.

I had named my truck Cassidy. She was a dependable, good-looking GMC Astro 95 with a Cummins 290 diesel engine. (Don't ask me why GM puts Cummins engines into their trucks when GM *makes* diesel engines.) Her odometer read 645,783 that morning, and every one of those miles was laid down by me. She's considered a total piece of shit by the freighthauler fraternity. They all want the long-nosed Peterbilts. Another disconnect between movers and freighthaulers is that movers don't much care what powerplant we drive so long as we're making money. The freighthaulers are the opposite. This is totally ludicrous to me, because it's not like they own what they drive. In my personal hierarchy, an owner-operator driving the junkiest old cornflake Mack is still miles ahead of a clockpuncher in a company-owned Pete. "Whatcha drivin'?" is a standard first question at truckstop coffee counters. "Got a bank account?" would be my first question.

Cassidy was running really well as I left Daytona, but she was not going to like the trip up north with an empty trailer. The further north you go, the rougher the roads get and an empty trailer bounces like crazy. Diesel engines want to work hard. What they like is a full load and a twenty-hour run at 65. They are phenomenal machines. When you get a good one and maintain it properly, which really only means keeping the oil clean and buying good fuel, you've got something that will run a million miles. There are five Class 8 (big-truck) diesel engine manufacturers in the United States: Cummins, which is the market leader, Detroit Diesel, which used to be GM but is now a division of Daimler, Volvo/Mack, PACCAR, and Caterpillar. They're all great, but the truckstop cowboys prefer the big Cats so they can wear the trucker hat that says DIESEL POWER. Engine manufacturers are different from truck makers. The Class 8 truck brands are Freightliner, Kenworth, Peterbilt, International, Volvo/Mack, and Western Star. All of them make excellent trucks, but Freightliner, also a division of Daimler, is far and away the industry leader. With the premium truck brands like Peterbilt or Western Star, a buyer is actually custom-ordering a vehicle. When you buy yourself a Peterbilt you order the engine, the transmission, the rear end, and any other features that you want, like an expanded wheelbase or a sliding fifth wheel. Petes are expensive because you're making a composite of the best features made by all the best manufacturers and putting it into what is probably the best truck chassis. I wouldn't know how to order one myself because I don't know a wheelbase from freebase. I'm a mover, not a gearhead.

———

I was running north in a convoy with nine other trucks through the interminable 199 miles of swamp, palmetto scrub, and south of the border signs that people call South Carolina. A convoy is a group of trucks traveling together. I don't get inside convoys very often because most trucks run too fast for me.

The front door of this convoy was a Bowman freighthauler

followed by three Armellini reefers hauling fresh flowers, then me, then a skateboard steel hauler, an Atlas bedbugger, another skateboarder hauling hot tubs, and the back door was a Schneider freight box called a "Pumpkin" because of its orange color. We flew together for 130 miles doing 65 the whole way. It was wonderful sitting in the cradle of the convoy. If the front door saw a gator in the road (gators are big pieces of tire tread on the roadway), he'd drawl "Gator" on his radio and pull into the hammer lane. I'd pull out after the Armellinis. We all fell into a groove. Everybody was driving well, everybody was professional, everybody was going fast but not crazy fast, and there was a plane of consciousness that we had together. It's the closest thing to a Zen experience I know, except when I'm in my loading trance. Both of those things are what keeps me out here. The rest of it is just hassle.

There was little chitchat on the radio. We exchanged CB handles and that was about it. My handle is U-Turn because I'm always in residential areas getting bad directions and have to reorient myself, often several times a day. The most common CB handles are Bandit, Lone Ranger, and Coyote. Willie Joyce's handle is Steamboat, and Tim Wagner's is Banknote.

I passed a bobtailer—a tractor without a trailer. Bobtailing tractors have a really weird look about them, kind of like a walrus out of the water. They're dangerous to drive, especially in wet weather, because the brakes are designed for a tractor *and* a trailer, so when you're bobtailing and hit the brakes hard, the tendency is for the truck to spin around.

This South Carolina stretch of I-95 is wallpapered with a zillion different billboards. The most common among them are the ones for SOUTH OF THE BORDER, simply the largest, tackiest, tourist trap in the Milky Way.

One thing South Carolina does have is an excellent public

radio system. From any point in the state you can pick a station up. The two best public radio networks are in South Carolina and Maine. Virginia is a mess. I understand why that happened in Maine, but South Carolina? Given the rest of its atavistic infrastructure, it's a mystery. There's absolutely nothing there. Once in a while I'll see someone fishing from a bridge but that's it. There doesn't appear to be a lot of opportunity for blacks, or whites for that matter, in rural South Carolina. Get a few miles off the highway and it's hard to believe you're in the United States. It looks more like South Africa. One of the things I like about the moving business is its equal opportunity attitude. The work is so hard and held in such low esteem that there's not a lot of room left over for bigotry. Anyone who will do this job is accepted. This did not go unnoticed by a large group of black men who flocked to the industry in the 1960s as long-haul drivers. North American Van Lines was proudly nicknamed North African Van Lines because it had so many black drivers. Just about the time I got on the road these guys were starting to retire, but I did get to know quite a few of them. Every one of them owned his own home and had put money away for retirement. I knew two who had second homes in Florida. They had nothing but good things to say about North American Van Lines and the moving business.

———

Once I made it through the gauntlet of SOUTH OF THE BORDER signs and reached the North Carolina border, it was fifty miles to Fayetteville, home of Fort Bragg—Fayettenam, as it's known, because it's the home of the 82nd Airborne and was one of the main clearinghouses for anyone heading over to Southeast Asia in the 1960s and '70s. I've done a lot of work there over the years. Right in the center of town they've got the 1832 Market

House, where slaves were bought and sold up until 1865. Orbiting the market for miles in all directions you have the typical economic support system for an American military town. That means pawn shops, secondhand car dealers, pawn shops, secondhand furniture dealers, secondhand clothing stores, pawn shops, gun stores, all-you-can-eat cafeterias, and, oh God, how could I forget, mobile homes and prefab home sales. Then you run the gamut of strip clubs and bowling alleys.

It's the pawnshops that give me pause. I've moved a bunch of military folks—nobody moves people around like the military—and they're no different from their countrymen in wanting the car, the house, the big TV, the guns, and the sound system. Just like their countrymen, they want it all, right now, today if possible. It's the American way, but military people don't make enough money to have it all right now, or actually . . . ever. That's one part of it. The other part of it is they have kids, lots of them, way more kids than families in the civilian world have, so that eats even further into their disposable income. In addition to that you have to factor in young enlisted men; I mean who else goes to strip clubs, right? (OK. Wrong. Lots of middle-aged truckers go to strip clubs.) Many of these these young enlisted folks get married young, aren't used to a steady income, and are easy prey for salesmen banging on their doors. The signs on the mobile home lots all say that if you come in with a military ID there's no credit check, no down payment, easy terms. Ergo, all the pawnshops. A pawnshop is a ruthless indicator of flawed financial planning. When you encounter a galaxy of pawnshops, like in Fayetteville, you don't need to be Lord Keynes to figure out what's going on.

When you move people and pack their stuff, you see how people really live, not how they want the neighbors to *think* they live. Louise DeSalvo wrote in a book called *On Moving* that "packing is a full-scale life inspection." She's spot on. I get to see the filthy bathrooms, the dirty dishes, the eight-year-old in diapers, the empty booze bottles, everything. The intimacy is immediate and merciless. I don't ask for this and I take no voyeuristic pleasure from it. Well, occasionally I do, but not often. It's just part of the job. As a driver, I get to set my boundaries, but a shipper doesn't. Shippers sense this, and they react to it with various ineffective defensive strategies. The most common is to make the movers anonymous. This makes the revelation of their life contradictions irrelevant. Basic linguistics supports my view: *I'm waiting for the movers, The movers are here, The movers just left* . . . We're not real people. We get tagged and filed away as a nebulous group of anonymous wraiths in order to deemphasize the intimacy. Regardless of psychological gymnastics, we know what we see, and many of us learn from it. It's a rare mover who becomes a collector of anything. Even rarer is a mover who gets hung up on the "sentimental value" of objects. After more than three thousand moves I know that everyone has almost the exact same stuff and I certainly know where it's all going to end up. It's going to end up in a yard sale or in a dumpster. It might take a generation, though usually not, but Aunt Tillie's sewing machine is getting tossed. So is your high school yearbook and grandma's needlepoint doily of the Eiffel Tower. Most people save the kids kindergarten drawings and the IKEA bookcases. After the basement and attic are full it's off to a mini-storage to put aside more useless stuff. A decade or three down the road when the estate is settled and nobody wants to pay the storage fees anymore, off it all will go into the ether. This is not anecdotal. I know because I'm the guy who puts it all into the dumpster.

Movers are there at the beginning point of accumulation and all the points to the bitter end, so we tend to develop a Buddhist view of attachment. We do not covet your stuff. It's freight. We'll take the best care we can because you're paying for that and we're responsible for the damage claim. But we don't care on any other so-called higher level because no higher level actually exists. Sentimental value of stuff is a graven image and a mug's game. The only beneficiary is the self-storage guy. What my customers need to know is that it's not the stuff but the connection with people and family and friends that matters. Practically everyone I move gets this wrong.

Be nice to your movers. What we do care about is making your transition into a new life and place as easy as possible by being professional and sympathetic. I think that's a responsible job and a worthy occupation. When we're allowed to do that, which isn't often, because most people are more concerned about their crockpot than a proper transition to a new life, you'll find out that we're on your side. When people let that happen, they're always surprised, and they relax.

———

I entered Virginia and immediately upped my game. Truckers call Virginia the Communist State because of its strict enforcement of highway laws and the harsh state police. They're especially tough at the weigh stations. Everyone has seen weigh stations, but most people probably have only have a vague idea what they are. Here's how they work: The federal weight limit for Class 8 trucks (tractor-trailers) on interstate highways is 80,000 pounds. That's because the road surface is engineered to support that. An overweight vehicle stresses the road surface. Roadways are designed to last a certain amount of time, and an early breakdown of the road means higher unbudgeted expenditures. Municipal finance types hate overweight trucks for that reason, and they transfer that hate to their minions. In Virginia it's open season on trucks. Other states are less aggressive. All trucks are required to pull into all weigh stations or face a hefty fine. When I pull in, the scale has three platforms: one for the front axle, the second for the drive axles, and the third for the trailer axles. Each axle has its own weight limit in addition to the gross vehicle weight limit. If you're overweight there's a fine.

Weigh stations are operated by the state's Department of Transportation, and they'll also use the opportunity to check logbooks, truck maintenance reports, vehicle registrations, permits, insurance, and driver licensing. The regulations and compliance metrics get stricter every year, which is one reason I get on my high horse about the free-ranging trucker cowboy myth. There's nothing more regulated than a trucker hauling for a big company. (I was going through Kansas one time when a thunderstorm came through. You've never seen weird weather like a midsummer Kansas thunderstorm. I pulled into a rest area to wait it out and started chatting with a FedEx driver in the lobby. We hadn't talked for two minutes when his phone rang. It was a compliance operative from a call center in Mumbai: "You've been redlined for making an unauthorized stop. What's going on?" They had his truck on GPS. All FedEx trucks are on GPS. It's getting even worse. Now some big freighthauling companies have 24/7 video in the cab. That ain't Wild West freedom, folks, that's Big Brother.)

You hear a lot these days about driverless cars, but what the people who run things really want are driverless trucks. It's the missing link. Loads are already operated robotically. When a driver pulls into certain distribution centers, he opens the door and a bunch of machines empty the trailer and put away the goods. His truck is then loaded by another cadre of machines. There's one warehouse guy making twelve bucks an hour watching computers and robots loading several dozen trailers. One guy is still one too many, though, and a couple dozen truck drivers waiting around is unacceptably inefficient. Real people will want health insurance and a living wage. Better to get rid of them entirely. No theft, no sick days, and no pensions.

Anyway, I always get nailed at Virginia weigh stations. If I loaded the nose of the trailer too tight I'd pop over the weight limit. The last time I was caught it was three in the morning at the Woodbridge weigh station on I-95 just south of DC. They're never closed, curse 'em. Generally if I'm over on my weight it means I have a lot of loads on, which means I'm in a hurry to try to get them off. So they pulled me in and kept me waiting. This Virginia trooper was really taking his time, and I was starting to fume. He finally wrote up his fine, and it turned out I was over 280 pounds on the drives and the fine was sixty-one dollars. I'm never over-weight by very much, so it's not like I'm destroying the roadway. The trooper handed me the receipt, and I said, "I hope you're real happy with the sixty-one dollars," He exploded. He put me up against the wall, yanked the wallet out of my pocket, pulled out my license, and called it in to see if it was clean. After thirty min-utes, the trooper returned my license, smiled, and said, "Well, driver, tell your trucker buddies what happens when you mouth off to a Virginia state trooper." I answered, "Yes sir, I will, sir."

Happy to leave Virginia behind, I cruised through Maryland and crossed into Delaware. The toll attendant (can you imagine a more anachronistic job?) looked like she was fourteen years old. I asked her if it wasn't past her bedtime, and she gave me a dirty look. Tollbooths are a particularly vexing aspect of truck driving. They tie up traffic and are completely unnecessary. We already pay to use the road through fuel taxes based on our weight and mileage, so they're double dipping besides slowing everything down.

The road was starting to get really bumpy and would get bumpier into North Jersey. Up through here you have to keep the seat belt cinched down real tight or you'll bang your head on the ceiling and knock yourself out.

My universe was firing on all cylinders as I pushed north on Interstate 95, putting Exit 12 Carteret/Rahway in North Jersey behind me. Yellow sodium arc lights from the factories, refineries, and warehouses discharged a murky, stagelit glow onto the gantry towers at Port Elizabeth. The horizon was broken by steel girders, steel cranes, steel storage tanks, steel trains, steel bridges, and steel ships. I had "Born to Run" blasting out from the oversize speakers, which sit on my sleeper mattress stuck to the back wall with strips of Velcro. (Last month in Miami I slammed on the brakes coming over the crest of a blind hill on the Southeast Expressway where the traffic was completely stopped. Both speakers hurled forward. One hit me on the back of my head, and the other cracked the right windshield. I've got two living-room-size Polk Audio speakers in the sleeper and two Visonik Little Davids sitting cozily on a pillow on the dashboard. Me being me, I replaced the windshield and put the speakers back on the Velcro, figuring I'd never have to slam on the brakes that hard ever again. Wrong.)

Coming into metro New York from points west or south has always supercharged me, but doing it in a big truck is pure adrenaline. This is the closest I ever come to feeling the true essence of life on the road. I've got a hard-muscled body, a big, comfortable, new tractor hauling a 53-foot moving trailer, grooving with my killer sound system, a 30-ounce Dr Cola in the holder. There's the whistle of the supercharger as I shift into thirteenth gear, the whoosh of the air dryer, my mouth slightly sour, arms shaking from the pounding of the wheel, making money, setting my own schedule, the Manhattan skyline on my right, flying fast and furious on my way up to home plate in Connecticut. I'm inside sixty miles of tremendously satisfying task saturation, what I call threading the needle. Me and the monster truck are hurtling through sixteen lanes of the most intense, dangerous, and exhilarating piece of roadway ever devised by man, and I'm the king of it all with my truck, my tunes, and my big independence. All the stories, the longings, the dreams, the books, the movies, the songs, the great American Dream of chucking it all and hitting the road? Well, right at this moment, I am the song.

These moments don't last long. Exhilaration will step aside and make room for the other reality that's always pushing to get in. Are these brief moments of euphoria worth the punishing loneliness, the physical abuse, and the lack of direction my job entails? Right now the answer is yes. Tomorrow morning, after three hours of fitful sleep, when I wake up shivering in the cold sleeper and stagger into a truckstop looking at another frozen burrito for breakfast, the answer will be no. My ambivalence, after almost ten years doing this, is starting to coalesce. Sometimes I can see the end coming but I'm stuck. Something will need to happen that will break me out. Some days I pray for that. I guess I'm not the master of my ship after all. Is that maturity, or is that resignation?

I parked my rig at 2 a.m. at the Callahan Bros. warehouse. I'd driven 1,095 miles in a little over twenty-two hours.

The next morning I was awakened by a loud bang against the side of my truck. I jerked up completely disoriented and terrified. I opened the curtain a slit, looked in my mirror, and saw Little Al at the tail end of my trailer holding a two-by-four like a baseball bat and giving me the finger. I had no idea where I was until I looked out the other side and saw I was parked in the Callahan Bros. yard along the fence rail under the drinking tree. Al was walking back to his straight truck, laughing. It was ten minutes after eight on a fucking Sunday morning.

I didn't find Little Al's wake-up call funny. I felt like ripping him to pieces, but since it was Little Al, who had been my mentor, I didn't. Since I was in my sleeper and naked, I lurched over and mooned the crew as they drove past. They'll be telling that one under the tree on Monday.

I got dressed and walked past Dan's Service Station over to the Callahan office. John was there checking to make sure Little Al's crew took off before going to church. John looked up from his desk and smiled.

"How's it going, fella? I thought you were in Florida." John never knew where I was.

"That was yesterday."

"You need anything?"

"I need some cartons and a few pads. I'm heading up to Vermont today and loading back to Florida. I was hoping to get some cash."

"How much do you want?"

"Three thousand."

"I'll be right back." A couple of minutes later John returned and handed me thirty Ben Franklins. "You know you've got a lot more than that in your account. I think it's about forty thousand dollars. What do you want me to do with it?"

"Hang on to it for now. I'll just load the equipment and head out."

"Are you OK, Murph? You've been running pretty hard."

"I'm OK, John. Just tired. See you later." That was my stop at home plate.

———

Thirty-six miles south of White River Junction, Vermont, on I-91, I was running an easy 65 up and down the hills. It was a lovely afternoon. There was the Connecticut River on my right and to my left a forest, then a patch of pasture, and a white farmhouse with a red barn. I saw a green sign that read SCENIC VIEW 1 MILE, so I slowed down to get off and take a look. Then I saw the next sign: NO TRUCKS. So much for seeing the country in a tractor trailer.

Vermonters have a totally different way of looking at life than the strip mall desert denizens of Florida. There's a Yankee stubbornness the way the farms are built into the hillsides and the way they all keep a certain distance from each other. It must be hell trying to make a living off this land. It's odd how Vermont's topography and geography are so pleasant and it's such a nice climate, but practically nobody lives here. Florida, which has a depressive climate and no topography, has people flocking there.

In St. Johnsbury I needed directions to the agent's office, so I pulled into a general store. The blight of the Quik Stop and Kum & Go hasn't completely infected New England yet, though I've no doubt it will. The woman inside was reading *Buddenbrooks*. I disturbed her. You definitely would not find a store clerk reading Thomas Mann in South Carolina. As I walked out eating a strawberry shortcake ice cream bar, this little kid looked at me, then my truck, and gave me the victory sign: "Go, trucker, go!" Good old Vermont.

Chapter 5
SEVEN SHIPPERS

M oving is a risky and capricious industry. Moving companies and the people who own them are a conservative bunch, equally impervious to the grandiose aspirations of charlatans and to the self-serving dreams of the solid citizens who constitute their customer base. Companies that have risen above the subsistence level of a laborer with a truck are open boats tossing about in economic high seas. The business at this level is cyclical, capital intensive, and seasonal. That's a particularly nasty combination bound to inculcate a certain degree of caution for those whose desire is to pass assets on to succeeding generations. Because of this innate caution, many of the early drayage companies are still around today: Wells Fargo began in 1852, Reebie Moving in Chicago in 1880, Holman in New Jersey in 1886, Security Storage of Washington, DC, in 1890, Bekins in Sioux City in 1891; countless others are still around and thriving. Wells Fargo of course, has moved on. Only 7 percent of all moving companies have more than fifty employees, 40 percent have fewer than five, and 96 percent are privately held. Another anomaly is the number of multigenerational families in the industry. Morgan

Manhattan in New York City is a perfect and not at all uncommon example. Morgan was founded in 1851 by Patrick Morgan, an immigrant from Ireland, who got hold of a horse and wagon and started hauling household goods. Today Morgan Manhattan is a multimillion-dollar moving conglomerate still owned and operated by the Morgan family.

The industry goes much further back than the nineteenth century. Short-haul moving was well developed in Europe and America in colonial times. The picture of a drayman with his horse and wagon brimming with furniture is a familiar one. A bit later we'll have large companies like Russell, Majors, and Waddell running the Pony Express and consolidating wagon trains from St. Louis for the trek out west. These companies collected fees from the dreamers, town boosters, religious whackos, misanthropes, psychopaths, and real estate hucksters who populated the immutable myth Americans call "the Winning of the West." The wagon train companies were actually primitive van lines, and the man in charge of the wagon train was the latter-day long-haul driver. Even today, the sleekest $60,000 moving trailer is essentially only a wagon, and the most modern $150,000 tractor is still rated in horsepower.

Today's moving companies grew in tandem with the development of trucks and roads in the early twentieth century. Up until about 1920, all long-distance moving was handled by railroads. Someone moving from New York to Chicago in 1900 would be better off selling everything and packing a suitcase. (It's still the best way.) A household move back then required a shipper to contract with a drayage company at origin to pack everything in wooden barrels and crates and cart them to the station. There the railroad men would load everything into a boxcar for the trip to Chicago. Upon arrival, the shipper would contract with another drayage company to load the goods onto a wagon, deliver to the residence, and uncrate and unpack.

If you think moving is expensive and a hassle now, back then it was a nightmare. This is a point I'd like to emphasize: Moving today is cheaper, safer, and performed better than at any time in history. Let's go back fourteen thousand years to our forebears crossing the land bridge in the Bering Sea. Moving was a dice-roll with death.

Sure, nowadays, every once in a while, something gets broken or lost. So? Nobody's getting ambushed and cut to pieces on a frozen mountain pass. Nobody's being forced to eat their mother-in-law due to a lack of forage. Nobody's getting their wagonload of household goods set on fire by hostile natives. I'm a careful mover. I respect people's stuff, but shit happens. You know why? *Because you're moving it.* Leave the piano in the living room for three generations. It will be fine. You want to put it somewhere else, guess what? You're taking a risk. Did you ever move your leg the wrong way and spend two weeks in a brace? Ever drop a cell phone in a toilet? Ever move a sofa to vacuum underneath and put a scratch on the floor? Most of us have done at least one of those things. I've done all those things. What I don't understand is why, when a mover scratches a floor or dents a lampshade, it's a justification for a ferocious freak-out at the entire industry. A quick lap around the internet will illustrate the dismal opinion of the moving industry by its customers. Most of it is vitriol, and some of it is, literally, insane. People go crazy when something happens to their stuff. The reaction, it appears to me, is generally overblown and not commensurate with the perceived offense.

Here's some perspective: The number three cause of death in the United States is medical error. Do doctors get vilified like movers? No. Some doctor gives you the wrong med, or the wrong dose, or the wrong diagnosis, and before you know it, you're lying in a coroner's fridge wearing a toe tag. This happens to hundreds of thousands of people every year, but people still go around in hushed tones deferring to *"the Doctor."* Nobody goes on the internet to spew bile about how Dr. X killed his wife.

And another thing, while I'm at it: The moving industry is often portrayed as this monolithic leviathan conspiring to separate as much money from its customers as it can grab. This *monolith* is actually thousands of individual enterprises, each with its own ideas about ethics and service. In truth, the moving industry is less like a leviathan and more like the Lebanese parliament. Each faction is vainly striving to achieve hegemony over its neighbors in an endless sequence of shifting alliances, treachery, and occasional benevolence.

Up until the Great Depression, the trucking industry was unregulated. Anyone owning a truck could carry any product anywhere for whatever price he could negotiate. As the depression deepened, the major players in trucking petitioned the government for help. In 1935, Congress regulated all interstate motor transportation, setting up a centralized schedule of fees and essentially closing the industry to new entrants. For the next forty-five years, interstate trucking rates were contrived by Byzantine formulas cooked up in the smoke-filled back rooms of trucking-industry trade associations.

The one exception was farm products. Transportation of farm products remained unregulated under the Agricultural Exemption of the 1935 law for two reasons. First was that American farmers wouldn't stand for it. They'd already experienced the benefits of a government-sponsored cartel in the form of the railroads. Farmers had seen enough central planning, thank you very much, at least insofar as it related to transportation. That isn't to say farmers didn't want New Deal help in the form of price supports, because they did; they just didn't want any other industries getting support. The second reason was the Roosevelt administration's dilemma of how to keep food prices low for the general population while simultaneously boosting farm incomes. The only way to do both was to lower costs in the supply chain (i.e., transportation). The contradiction here is that while it was considered in the national interest to protect large trucking companies throughout the nonfarm economy, it was also considered in the national interest to keep agricultural trucking small and fragmented.

This two-tiered trucking world is what spawned the trucker culture that exists to this day. Your hourly driver is a union man, or a company man, anyway. He's paid a wage, is home most of the time, and has a pension plan, health insurance, and vacations. He's the direct descendant of the regulatory system. Your independent driver is a private contractor. He leases or finances his own truck, is probably from a rural area of the Midwest, or Deep South, and is driving a truck because he can't make a living farming, won't work in a factory, and refuses to punch a time clock. He's the direct descendant of the Agricultural Exemption system. The latter group is the culturally dominant one, and the hourly boys take all their cues from the gypsies. Everything from the ubiquity of country music to the cowboy hats and belt buckles, right down to the food in whatever restaurants are left, are remnants of the anti-urban, anti-statist, anti-union origins of the wildcat drivers of the 1930s and '40s. I personally find the whole thing maddeningly idiotic, as the gypsies would be the biggest beneficiaries of a bit of cartelization. As it stands now, most of them are over-the-road sharecroppers feeding their labor into the insatiable maw of Big Ag, which is happy enough to let them keep their cowboy myth in return for keeping all the money.

Almost all long-haul movers are in the second group, as am I. I lease my truck, I set my own schedule, and my revenue is subject to the shifting winds of each load.

——

I loaded my first shipment for this Florida trip in Lyndonville, Vermont, north of St. Johnsbury in the early morning. My first shipper's name was Murray, and it was 1,000 pounds going to Kendall, Florida. It was a mini shipment, maybe thirty pieces or so, and I loaded it at the warehouse which was one of the now unused hangers at Lyndonville's defunct airport. The road to it was the runway. This was the smallest North American agent I'd been to. The guy who owned it was an ex-long-haul driver taking a shot at owning his own business. I wished him well but didn't have high hopes.

My second pickup was in a town called Marshfield. I encountered a low bridge outside of town. I didn't get much of a warning. The sign that said LOW CLEARANCE AHEAD 13 FEET was only twenty yards from the bridge. My trailer runs 13'4", but I squeaked under it, going slowly with my head out the window looking backward. Truckers call hitting a low bridge "getting a haircut." So far I've avoided that travesty. I haven't used a runaway truck ramp either. Yet.

This shipment was another 1,000-pound mini belonging to Mr. and Mrs. Howell, who were moving to Largo. They were a charming elderly couple. When I arrived it was just noon, so they invited me to sit down with them for lunch. They served homemade Vermont pickled beets, turkey salad sandwiches, and hot tea. They told me they had come to Marshfield from Worcester, Massachusetts, in 1957 when they bought the general store. Mrs. Howell said the locals were at first suspicious of them, being as they were from out of town, and worse from out of state, and worse from the Deep South, i.e., Massachusetts. After more than forty years in Marshfield they were giving up on winter and snowbirding south. The Howells had bought a double-wide trailer in a retirement park. I hoped they would adjust well down there. It's true that winters in Florida are mild, but the rest of the year it's a blazing inferno.

I picked up two more little ones, a Mr. Gross and a Mr. Warren, at a warehouse in Essex Junction and started the three-hundred-mile trudge to Bangor. When you're a dispatcher sitting in a cube in Indiana, New England looks pretty small, but it isn't. There are no east/west interstates and my trek on US Route 2 took forever. I went up and over the White Mountains, through New Hampshire and into Maine, breezing through one dead or dying town after another. I hit Dysart's Truck Stop in Bangor at 3 a.m. and crawled into the sleeper. Five hours later I arrived at Central Maine Moving & Storage on the dot of 8 a.m. Of course nobody was there. This was another one of those weird agents I enjoy going to. This place wasn't a regular warehouse either; it was an old elementary school. Someone finally showed up around eight fifteen, and while I waited for the paperwork, I sat down in one of those school desks like we had in seventh grade. The classrooms were used as storage units. I kept expecting a bell to go off and see some nun fingering a detention slip and asking me what I was doing.

I had called this agent a few days ago to arrange for some help. They gave me one of their regular guys and told me to pay him twelve dollars an hour. I picked up the bill of lading and directions, and we drove off to South Bangor to load 3,000 pounds belonging to Mr. and Mrs. Taylor, who were moving to Naples, Florida. Mr. Taylor had sold his accounting business the year before, and part of the deal was that he had to stay awhile and help them operate it. Now he was moving from a three-story Victorian into a ranch house on a golf course.

My helper's name was Warren Pease, I swear to God. He was a thorough professional, and we loaded the Taylors in no time.

One of the dirty secrets of the moving business is that a shipper has no idea what kind of human offal a driver might pick up for day labor. Often I can pick up help from the local agent, but not always. At truckstops there are always guys dangling around looking for a day's work; they're what we call lot helpers. I can't get from my truck to the fuel desk at any truckstop in the country without some guy asking, "Hey, driver, you need any help today?" Sometimes they even bang on the truck and wake me up. It can be very annoying or very useful depending upon my labor requirements, though banging on the side of a truck is never a good idea. It's a great way to get a bullet in the head. Over the years I've been reduced to picking up help in soup kitchens, parole offices, and the corner bar.

The higher-end work I do now requires my laborers to have passed a background check, and their names have to be on file with the van line. No longer can I just pick up a guy from the truckstop who may or may not ransack your medicine cabinet to score your expired Oxycontin. I've got a little black book with the names of top-notch, executive-class movers in forty-eight states. I don't give out those names to anyone because these guys are well-paid professionals in high demand.

———

This trip had me in a daze. Normally I'll run with three, maybe four shipments. This time I had seven; two of them entailed extra pickups and deliveries going to six different cities, ending in Key West. Most of the shipments were small, and I'd gotten them all mixed in with each other. They wouldn't be unloading in the sequence they went on, either, so I'd be digging some of them out. I knew I had to be empty on the Sunday of the last week of the month. Hardly anyone moves out of Florida except in a coffin. I've heard there's a mortician in New York who's cornered the market on snowbird cadavers. That's a shame. I could probably get two hundred coffins in the truck and get them up there before they started to stink too bad if the price was right. No damage claims, no crazy shippers.

I had three more to pick up after Bangor, so I headed south. I stopped at Hal's Truck Stop in Kittery to grab a shower. I fell asleep in the truckstop parking lot listening to *All Things Considered* on Maine Public Radio. Every driver I've ever encountered listens to public radio. The great thing about NPR is that when you lose one signal you can pick up another that continues the broadcast. Some may not like the slant, if there is one, though it would be incorrect to think that truckers constitute some harmonized bloc of redneck atavism. I've heard *All Things Considered* called *Small Things Considered* and *One Side Considered*, and even heard a Klan member from Georgia call it *US Jews and Girls Report*. (He might have been a bigot, but he was a listener.) If I can, I'll schedule my driving to catch *Fresh Air* with Terry Gross. She's got that omniscient NPR tone they all have, but she always has someone interesting on. I've got a little crush on Terry, actually. It's probably because I've spent more time with her than anyone else in my life.

At the fuel desk they gave me a towel for the shower. Most truckstops now have private showers, but this was Hal's in Kittery, not a gleaming Bosselman's out on I-80 west of the big ditch. Hal's had one large shower room with six spigots, like in high school, and there was a coin slot next to each spigot. You put in a quarter and that bought you five minutes' worth of hot water. If you wanted more, you put in more money. Where was I supposed to put my quarters? I ended up thumbing them into my bar of soap. Though communal, the shower and bathroom stalls were spotless. There weren't any glory holes drilled between the stall walls like you see down south.

I was about to jump into the shower when another guy came in. It didn't bother me unduly, but I would have preferred to shower alone. This fellow had his clothes in a clear plastic bag: new jeans, new briefs, and a three-pack of pocket T-shirts. He saw me looking at the bag.

"Now don't get all edgy there, driver. I'm no hobo. I drive for Pottle's out of Bangor. I got fired yesterday, supposedly for too many fender-benders. I went in there today to pick up my CB and fuzzbuster and damn if they didn't rehire me. Guess they wanted to teach me a lesson . . . more likely they had a hot load they couldn't cover. They're good folks, actually, and I can be a pain in the ass. I hadn't brought any extra clothes, seeing as I was fired, so when they dispatched me to Tucson an hour ago I had to bobtail to the Kmart and pick up some fresh threads. Shit. I just remembered I took a chicken breast out of my freezer to eat tonight. Left it in the sink at home. Oh well." He stuck out his hand. "I'm Lone Ranger, who are you?"

"U-Turn."

"Glad to know you. I forgot about this gumball-machine shower setup. How about you float me a couple quarters out of that bar of soap? I'll pay you back outside. The real reason they fired me was because I took off the month of August to go fishing. I sure do love trucking. A man can quit whenever he wants and always find another job."

He went on like that throughout the shower. Lone Ranger gave me his entire job history, all the while jacking my quarters.

He was the real deal trucker/drifter type. I liked him because he was intelligent and good-natured. He just had this streak of independence that kept his life flirting with the breadline. When that line got crossed, like today, he went happily to the Kmart and rolled with it.

After my shower, I bought thirty gallons of go-go juice for the fifty-mile hop over to Manchester, New Hampshire, and went to sleep. I love sleeping in my sleeper, and I sleep better there than anywhere else. Getting up wasn't nearly as pleasant; the cab was chilly, even with the heat on, and it's always a struggle to wriggle into clean clothes in the cramped space. I had to piss real bad too. I took care of that with an empty Gatorade bottle stowed for the purpose. (Truckstop parking lots are littered with flattened Gatorade bottles, and a hot summer afternoon will provide a memorable olfactory experience.) I climbed out of the rig and was in Ray the Mover's office at seven thirty ready to pick up paperwork and my two lumpers. The plan was to load 4,000 pounds out of Milford, New Hampshire, for Beverly Hills. I got my paperwork at five minutes to nine, the pricks, and the dispatcher told me to follow the two packers out there because the packing hadn't been done yet. I wasn't getting a good feeling.

We arrived at the residence a little before ten. Not good. The packers I was following got lost, of course.

The shipper was an elderly woman named Mrs. Fowler. When we got inside the house, we saw that she hadn't done a thing to prepare for her move. Mrs. Fowler had told the agent she was going to do all the packing except for a bedroom mirror, her mattresses, and some dishes in the kitchen. We had to force open the front door of the house because there was so much crap in the way. She'd lived there for twenty years and apparently had thrown nothing away. We couldn't get any of the interior doors open either, because every single tabletop, chair, and floor area was piled high with newspapers, files, magazines . . . It was the most full house that I had ever seen in my life, and I've been a lot of years in this game.

"OK, Mrs. Fowler," I said, surveying this residential scree field, "why don't we go through the house and see what's going with us to Florida?" She took us into the first room and said that the only thing going was the lamp on the table.

"Good. What about the kerosene lamps on the wall?"

"Oh yes, they go too."

"How about the pictures on the wall?"

"Oh, the pictures? Yes, yes. The pictures go too."

"What about the stuff on the mantelpiece?"

"Oh, yes, yes. That's got to go."

"How about the bookcase? Is the bookcase going?"

"Yes, the bookcase is going."

"What about the books in it?"

"Oh, yes, yes. The books are going. Well, some of them are going."

"OK. Is there anything else in this room?"

"No, no. That's everything."

"What about the stuff inside the china cabinet?"

"Oh, of course, that has to go. I showed that to the other man."

I was still trying to be nice. This was our first room, and it was a big house, and I already knew what kind of day it was going to be.

"Ma'am, it's very important that we know exactly what goes and what doesn't, down to every little brass ring."

"Oh, well, I can get this stuff together as you people are working."

"I'm sorry, ma'am, it can't be done that way. I have to write up an inventory. We have to know what's going before we start."

She acquiesced to that and began bobbing her head happily. "OK. Let's go into the next room."

"Before we do that, what about the pitchforks on the wall? Do they go?"

"Oh, yes, yes. They go."

"Look, ma'am, would you look around, just in this room, and tell me exactly what's left that you haven't mentioned that's supposed to go?"

"That's everything."

"What about the television?"

"Oh, yes, that goes."

This went on all day from ten in the morning until nine that evening. I never did get a clear idea about what she was shipping. My inventory was a work of fiction. It was the most screwed-up, messy, filthy, disgusting move I'd had. The packers were slow, of course. They were milking it. Lucky for me I had picked up a bunch of packing material at Callahan's. I loaded the entire truck myself: dressers, desks, boxes, chairs, tables, end tables, night stands, appliances, everything. By eight thirty that night I had completely filled my trailer. Mrs. Fowler was still rummaging through closets when I went upstairs.

"Look, ma'am, you've got to stop now."

"What do you mean?"

"The truck is full. I can't take anything else."

"What about the rest of my things?"

"They'll send another truck and bring the rest down to Florida later."

She brightened at this. "Oh, good, then I can get the rest of my things ready then."

"Absolutely," I replied. "Ma'am, I hope you understand that every one of these boxes we're packing is costing an average of twenty dollars apiece for the box and thirty dollars for the labor to pack it."

"Really? I thought the other man put the packing on the estimate."

"He did. He put three mattress cartons, one mirror carton, and three dishpack cartons on the estimate. We packed that in the first twenty minutes. You're looking at another two thousand dollars in packing and another six thousand in extra weight."

"I didn't know it worked that way."

"It does work that way. Do you think all this extra work is free?"

The irony here was that this whole fiasco was going to work out extremely well for me, if not for anyone else. She didn't have a binding estimate, so all the packing and extra weight would be added to her bill. My truck was full, and I'd picked up an extra couple of grand on packing and material. I wouldn't be able to load in Newburgh or make the extra stop in Rhode Island either. All told, my schedule had been reduced by one full day with more revenue than anticipated.

I pulled into the Secondi Bros. truckstop in Connecticut to get my gross weight at 1 a.m. I filled up with fuel first to bump the weight of her shipment. A gallon of diesel weighs slightly over 7 pounds, and I put in 140 gallons. Fowler's load came in at 12,260 pounds. It had been estimated at 4,000 pounds. That's over six tons of stuff manually carried and loaded by me, though to be perfectly accurate, I probably shouldn't count the 1,000 pounds of diesel she'll be billed for. Serves her right.

I mixed a large Dr Cola at Secondi's and headed south. It's only sixty miles to the George Washington Bridge, and I wanted to get across to beat the morning traffic. I did a little math on the Cross Bronx Expressway. I'd worked seventy-three hours in five days. That's just the way I liked it. As the Grateful Dead sang somewhere, "Too much of everything is just enough."

I couldn't get Lone Ranger out of my mind. He was a happy man, though he had little in the way of material wealth except his modest new wardrobe. I kept thinking about the thawing chicken breast he'd left in his sink. It might be six months before he got home again. For him, that was a problem for another time. Lone Ranger didn't attack life every day with judgment, resistance, and a perpetual chip on his shoulder. (They say a well-balanced Irishman is a man with a chip on both shoulders.) He was the perfect Zen truck driver, taking it all in and enjoying every moment. I was the opposite. I envied him. A lot. What he didn't have, and what I had in abundance, was anger. I had it when I started out as a mover and I had it when I became a driver. I had brilliantly managed to select a career where frustration was the norm. That allowed me to to justify remaining angry all the time. The truck broke down, the traffic sucked, my helpers were lazy, the shippers were paranoid, and my van line exploited me. In my rare leisure moments, which mostly took place in pool halls and truckstops, everyone around me was angry too. Something didn't feel right about that but as long as I had loads I didn't have to think about it. I'd been angry so long I didn't know how to feel any other way.

Chapter 6
THE POT OF GOLD

For a long time I used to have a helper in Florida named Tommy Mahoney. Since he didn't haunt truckstops or moving-company loading docks, he wasn't strictly a lot helper. In fact, he'd have taken enormous Irish umbrage at that term. He'd probably have called himself an on-call professional. He didn't have a regular job, but the stable of road drivers who knew him kept him pretty busy. He'd make between $150 and $250 a day, so in a good week he'd make well over $1,500, plus tips. All cash and tax-free. Then again, on a bad week he'd make nothing.

Tommy loved Irish music, bluegrass, and primitive country, and he'd go out every night to coffeehouses to keep up to date. One of the things that made him so odd is that he never slept. Ever. He once told me that when he lived in New York he worked night shifts at the A&P and stopped sleeping one day. It sounds incredible, but I traveled with him for days, sometimes a week, and he really never slept. Because of that I called him the Vampire, but he was known all over the country among road drivers as Brooklyn Tom. I once asked him why, seeing as he was from

Queens. He told me that as soon as people heard him talk his New York street accent they just assumed he was from Brooklyn. "These monkeys around here don't know Brooklyn from Queens, so I let it ride."

I'd arranged for Tommy to meet me at the first delivery drop in Florida. My schedule was to unload Fowler, Howell, and Gross on Friday and Taylor, Warren, and Murray on Saturday. This would give me Sunday to rest, clean up the trailer, and be ready to load Monday. It was perfect, the first workday of the last week of the month. If there was a pot of gold to be taken out of the sandpit, I'd be properly positioned for it.

———

I crossed the George late Wednesday night and pulled into the Vince Lombardi rest area to sleep. The Vince is a notorious pickle park, and that night the place was swarming with sleeper leapers, so I rolled down to Bordentown Junction and slept there. That was Wednesday. I drove all day and night Thursday and hit Beverly Hills at 3 a.m. Friday.

The first delivery was Mrs. Fowler, the hoarding artiste from New Hampshire, who was supposed to have 4,000 pounds and ended up with 12,000. Her estimated cost of services had been $4,000 for her move. Ray the Mover told me that Mrs. Fowler had prepaid her full bill of $11,967. How about that? Almost triple the estimate. The extra charges will no doubt spawn another "Tale of Horror from the Moving World," but it was entirely her own fault. She was not truthful about how much stuff she was moving. Moving stories, like losing virginity stories, have a universal one-upmanship quality about them. Bring up the subject anywhere, anytime, and a randomly selected heretofore reasonable human being will launch into a rabid tale of premeditated malfeasance, only to be outdone by an adjacent interlocutor retailing even more heinous crimes.

I arrived at Mrs. Fowler's at 8 a.m. The property manager was waiting for me. Good old Mrs. Fowler. The lovely woman had bought a ground-floor condo. I discovered I'd given Tommy bad directions, so he was going to show up late and pissed off. He's pretty smart, but when you are dealing with directions the key is to stop, figure it out, and don't go anywhere until you know exactly where you're going. Here's a useful tip about directions: Never ask a convenience store clerk, never ask someone loitering on the street, and never ask anyone over sixty-five years of age.

Tommy wasn't there yet, but I set up the walkboard. It went right inside the front door. No stairs, no long carries, no elevator, and, best of all, no Mrs. Fowler. Tommy showed up at eight thirty with steam coming out of his hairy Irish ears.

"Hello, Tommy. I'm sorry about the directions, but your luck just changed. I've got the walkboard inside the house, it's all on one floor, and all we have to do is wheel everything in. No stairs, no climbing, no lifting, no crazy shipper. If this got any easier I'd ask you to pay me."

"Fuck you" was his greeting. "I'll never meet a driver again at residence. If you want to use me you can goddam well pick me up."

"I wasn't going to drive two hundred miles out of my way to pick you up, Tommy. I don't care how good you are."

"It's a hundred miles. Don't exaggerate."

"It's a hundred down to get you and a hundred back. That's two hundred, Einstein. Besides, if I'd known how pissy you'd be and how easy this delivery would be, I'd have done it myself. You could still be home bitching at your wife instead of at me."

The property manager took off, saying to call him if we needed anything. Mrs. Fowler's delivery took two and a half hours, which is really fast for 12,000 pounds. It took me almost twelve hours to load it. We sort of guessed which room stuff would go into, and we didn't worry too much about getting it wrong. Mrs. Fowler probably wouldn't notice if her beds were set up in the kitchen. We did the best job we could and took off after the property manager signed off that everything had been delivered. He had no idea, but the papers were signed, the van line was paid, and there would be no damage claim. In my world, that's a successful move.

I'd gotten one load off out of the six I had on board, and it was the biggest one. The only thing on my mind was my scheduled call to Gary in dispatch at the end of the day. I was still crossing my fingers for the pot of gold.

Largo came off smoothly. This was Mr. and Mrs. Howell's stuff from Marshfield. The Howells weren't in Florida yet, so the trailer park manager let us in. The Howells had one of those ancient, dark wooden bedroom sets with a bureau, double dresser, vanity with mirror, and bed with a big headboard and footboard. It looked funereal stuffed into the trailer's master bedroom. Mrs. Howell's church organ looked like a giant cockroach in the living room. We finished in about ten minutes, and the manager signed off on the inventory. Papers signed, van line paid, no damage claim.

Sarasota was our next stop. Route 19 south to St. Pete and then over Tampa Bay via the dual spans of the Sunshine Skyway Bridge. I've been on the road so long I remember driving the Sunshine Skyway right after a freighter hit it in 1980 and knocked half the southbound span into the water, taking with it six cars, a truck, and a Greyhound bus. Thirteen people were killed. They used the remaining span for both northbound and southbound traffic until 1987. It was narrow, congested as hell, and the northbound traffic was right next to you with no median. That was scary enough, but it got really hairy at the top—it's a high bridge because all the tankers and military ships need clearance into Tampa, and at the top was the dangling steel of the other span as it opened into the abyss. Freaky.

As we crested the bridge, Tommy, in the shotgun seat, started cutting a lime for the first of his many daily vodka and cranberry cocktails. He kept his supply in a big thermos at the bottom of his duffle bag. I was annoyed at Tommy because we still had work to do. The unwritten rule was *No drinking until the workday is over*. I'd have to write the unwritten rule. The unfortunate truth was that to get the quality help I need, I have to make allowances or I'll have nobody at all.

We came off I-75 just south of Sarasota to deliver Mr. Gross. We headed west off the ramp and had driven maybe a mile when the road simply ended. But wait; there was the billboard, there was the security shed, there was the golf course, and there was the right turn into Whispering Pines, Palmetto Groves, Majestic Manor, Golden Gables, Century Village, Martin Downs, Sunburn Acres, Twin Beavers, or Sunset Farts. Who gives a shit? It's the same old Florida crap. However these places get named, rest assured, the more lyrical the moniker, the more of a sunblasted, cookie-cutter nightmare the place will be.

This one looked solidly middle-class because the security shed was unmanned and the gate was open. At least it wasn't a high-rise. I took a right into the development, and a tipsy Tommy Mahoney started languorously reading off street signs.

"Wren . . . Robin . . . Blue Jay . . . Cardinal . . . Oriole . . . Yankees . . . Red Sox . . ."

"Stop screwing around, Tommy, what street are we looking for?"

"Ostrich."

"Bullshit."

"Penguin."

"Tommy, I'm gonna throw your drunk ass out of this truck. What's the fuckin' street?"

"Kiwi."

"You asshole. Gimme the directions."

"You know something, Finn? You're really uptight sometimes. You should learn to relax."

"I'll relax when I find this guy's street. What's it called?"

"We passed it already. It was Oriole."

"We passed it! You slack fucker. Where am I gonna turn this thing around in this fuckin' rat's nest?"

"You're the guy who calls himself U-Turn. You're the guy who says he can turn a tractor-trailer around inside a car wash. Let's see you do your stuff."

"Tommy, why are you fucking with me right now?"

"Don't worry about it. This road goes all the way around. Oriole's just up on the right. The guy's house is on the left, we're unloading from the left. We're perfect. I've been in this stupid place before. It's hard to keep them separated. I didn't remember until I saw all the birds' names."

"You're fucked up. Are you in shape to work?"

"I ain't fucked up, just a little buzzed. You're the one who's fucked up."

"That's it. No booze until the working day is done, you got that?"

"Yes, massa, I got that. Here's Oriole. Turn right."

Mr. Gross was an obese man of about sixty. He was standing in front of the house waiting for us. Tommy jumped out. I put on the air brakes, shut off the engine, and hopped down.

"Mr. Gross, I presume? Hi. My name is Finn Murphy. How's it going?"

"Hi, Ken," he said. "Everything's going into the garage. Can't think why I shipped it. I got all new stuff when I moved down here."

"Yes. Everybody does that. We have to do a little paperwork before we unload."

"You mean you want the check."

"Yes, sir. A certified check for eighteen hundred dollars."

"That stuff isn't worth eighteen hundred dollars. I don't know what I'm going to do with it. How 'bout you keep it and I keep the dough? What am I going to do with an Ethan Allen living room set in Sarasota?"

"I dunno, Mr. Gross. Can we go inside and do the paperwork?"

"Sure."

Tommy started wheeling boxes into the garage while we went inside. Mr. Gross waddled over to the sideboard and poured himself a scotch.

"Want a drink, Ken?"

"No thanks, Mr. Gross. About that check . . ."

"I don't know what I'm doing down here, Ken." Mr. Gross topped off his drink with some water, "I had the largest commercial window-washing business in New England three months ago. We did all the big buildings in Portland, Burlington, Manchester, hospitals, schools—we had 'em all. Then one day this guy offered me a fortune to sell up if we did the deal fast. All cash. Before I could shake myself awake it was over. I was up there in Vermont freezing my ass off with nothing to do, so hell, buy a place in Florida, right?"

"Congratulations, sir. About that check . . ."

"Oh yeah, here." He handed me the certified check.

"Thanks. Say, Mr. Gross, could I use your phone?

"Sure, Ken."

This was the key call I'd been anticipating all week. I had waited to give Gary the most time to try to scrounge something out of Florida for Monday. To a dispatcher, success is defined by clearing freight off his board and doing it on schedule. He's not overly concerned with driver revenue. I'm not required to take loads dispatched to me, but if I get a reputation for refusing loads they'll all dry up, so everything revolves around a balance between Gary and me. He'll give me as much garbage as he thinks I'll haul, but he has to make it up sometimes and give me some gold. Gary's had some rotten shit I've hauled for him—overflows, cut-rate military, and short hauls nobody wanted. In my view, he was way overdue for a big payload. I called him at four forty-five Indiana time.

"Hey, Gary, it's Finn."

"Finn Murphy. Driver number 6-5-1-8. You know, I was thinking about cutting out early, and then I thought nope, 6518's going to be calling looking for a load out of Florida, and since I live for 6518, I'm going to stay here until it calls."

"TGIF, Gary. You're pretty jolly today. Is that because it's fifteen minutes to the weekend or is it the sound of my voice?"

"You do have a distinctive voice for a truck driver. You don't have a southern accent, and you speak in full sentences. Why is it that all truckers talk with a southern accent? I'm dispatching a couple guys from fucking Saskatchewan and they talk like the Dukes of Hazzard. What is that?"

"They're perpetuating a myth, Gary. A myth is a way of looking at life that doesn't exist, never did exist, but gives people a worldview they can understand and accept."

"My question was rhetorical, Finn. You missed the irony. You always do."

"Rhetorical? Irony? Those are pretty big words for a dispatcher. With all this chitchat, you've got really good news or really bad news. Which is it?"

"Lemme tell you a little story, 6518. Can I call you 65, to keep things on a first-name basis? 6518 sounds so formal. Just kidding, Finn, sort of. Do you have any idea of how many drivers I talk to every day? No, you don't. Sorry . . . It's quitting time and I'm getting punchy. You know how some of our agents are really small, like that Woodway place in Vermont? He's tiny, but he's exclusive to us. Other places have so little activity that one little moving company might be the agent for more than one van line. We don't like that, but in small markets it works for us."

"This is fascinating, Gary. Right now I'm looking for a load."

"Patience, youngster, patience. You're a young man in a hurry and that's not always a good thing to be. Anyway, one of these renegade agents is in Key West. He's the agent for Allied, United, Mayflower, us, everybody. The guy's name is Helmut. He's an island guy, more into fishing and boozing than working, but he's got a big warehouse, and there's not enough action for any competition, so he's got Key West locked up tight. Last week Helmut got called out to the Naval Air Station. There's an admiral with a couple days to retirement. The admiral is from Connecticut, his grown kids live in Connecticut, and he's going to live in Connecticut after he retires. Naturally, he doesn't want to pay to move his stuff from Key West, so—because he can—he transfers himself to Groton Navy Base outside New London. It's his last official posting, and even if he's only going to be posted there for five minutes, Uncle Sam will pick up the tab for the move. These military guys are no dummies. Got it so far, Finn?"

"Got it, Gary, great story. Does it have an ending?"

"Indeed it does, and you're going to like the ending, trust me. Helmut went out to the admiral's res and did the estimate. He couldn't decide whether to give the load to us, Allied, or United. Not being a guy to stress out about these things, he put off his decision. Come Monday, Helmut got busy and the admiral slipped his mind. The admiral continued to slip his mind until exactly eighteen minutes ago when the transportation officer on base called Helmut to check that everything was in order for the admiral on Monday. Helmut lied to the TO and said, 'Of course we're all ready for the admiral . . . Yessirree!' Helmut then started working the phones. I don't know who he called first, but we got it. Ya ready?"

"Ready."

9/26AM OA A1 Key West Shipper Clark GBL 21,000 lbs Pack and load Line haul $16,750 DA Whaling City Movers New London CT Delivery date 9/30.

"Wow, Gary, twenty-one thousand pounds. A full load, and packing. Nice work." I was automatically doing the sums in my head but couldn't get to a number. I was going to need a calculator. A true blue pot of gold. This *never* happens.

"Yeah. Normally we'd be fighting like cats over this in dispatch. There are at least twenty drivers empty in Florida, and some of 'em have been waiting more than two weeks. The thing is, the planners knew they had to get this thing assigned today and all the other drivers have checked in. I told the head planner you were in Miami and empty and would be calling in just before five. You are in Miami and empty, right?"

"Absolutely empty, Gary. I'm down here in Kendall just folding pads and cleaning up the truck." Actually I was in Sarasota with three shipments to deliver the next day.

"Good. So Charlie, the planner, looks around the dispatch room and says to me, 'If 6518 calls in before five, give it to him. We can't take any chances. The guy's a fucking admiral. If nobody shows up Monday he'll probably drop an artillery shell on Helmut's warehouse.'"

"Good story, Gary. Thanks. I owe you one."

"You owe me a bunch. Guess what else? The reason you're unloading the 30th is not only because the admiral retires that day, but also because your agent up there, Callahan Bros., booked an exclusive use from Westport, Connecticut, to Vero Beach loading on the first. Your name is on the ticket. So you're full going up and full going down. I won't have to talk to you for weeks."

"You'll miss my melodious unsouthern voice, you'll see."

"Not likely. Go take care of the admiral. I'll talk to you in October sometime."

"OK, Gary. Thanks again. Bye."

I couldn't believe my amazing luck. I had 21,000 pounds for Connecticut to pack and load starting Monday and an exclusive-use backup load after that going back down. This was going to be a net $25,000 month, my best turn ever. Freighthaulers who elbow me aside at truckstops and make fun of my chrome-free little Astro can eat my fumes. Fuckin' sharecroppers.

A pack and load was a rarity for me. It meant that I did the entire move from beginning to end. I didn't often get these super gravy loads because dispatchers saved them for their pet drivers. I do my job, but I'm no corporate ass-kisser swinging by Fort Wayne laying cases of Coors, Maine lobsters, or Virginia hams at the feet of those who control my fate.

I went outside. Tommy was wheeling in the last two end tables of the Ethan Allen set. It was nice stuff, but Mr. Gross was right. It had no business being down here. We went inside to say good-bye. Tommy followed me, not to say good-bye but to be on the spot in case we got a tip.

"I've got the inventory sheet, Mr. Gross. Do you want to check it off and make sure it's all here?"

"Nah. I'm sure it's all here."

"I'm sure it is too. Want to sign right here, then?"

"OK."

"That's it, Mr. Gross, we're all set. Anything else we can do?"

"You sure you boys won't have a drink?"

"No thanks," I said quickly. Tommy, I was well aware, would certainly have a drink. "We've got to drop another load tonight in Naples."

"Tonight? Naples? You're working hard. I used to work hard. Enjoy it, boys. You never know, you might miss it when it's over." He reached into his wallet and handed Tommy a ten and me a twenty.

"So long, Mr. Gross. And thanks."

The paperwork was done, I had the check, and there would be no claim. Mission accomplished. As I made the left on Blue Heron Way back to I-75, I caught a final glimpse of Mr. Gross standing at the end of his driveway with his right hand in the air and the left clutching his scotch.

We were not actually delivering in Naples that night but the next morning. I had an easy two-hour run south on the beautiful, spanking-flat I-75. I was cruising along at an easy 65 when I was passed by a motorcycle. I didn't see him in my mirrors and didn't know he was there until he passed me. I would never ride a motorcycle on an interstate. I can barely see motorcycles, ever. Truckers call them murdercycles, and riders are called organ donors. One time on I-90 in eastern Washington I was in the left lane passing another truck and a motorcycle came right between the two of us doing about 90. He had maybe a foot of clearance on either side of two semis both doing over 70.

I took out Mr. Gross's twenty and handed it to Tommy. "Here you go. You know I always give my tips to the lumper." I've got this weird prejudice that a driver shouldn't accept tips.

"Thank you," he said, and reached for his thermos of Cape Codders.

We got to Naples a little after eight. There was a strip center outside of town where I always parked. There's nothing resembling a truckstop in pretty little Naples. The shopping center had a Laundromat, a liquor store, an IHOP, a Kmart, and, best of all, a Chinese restaurant. There was a North American truck there already, plus an Allied and a Mayflower. I pulled up next to them. It was starting to look like a truckstop in pretty little Naples now. Normally I'd go over and talk to the drivers, but since I had a full load out of Key West for Monday, I didn't. The North American guy might be one of those drivers who's been waiting two weeks to load, and if he heard about my 21,000 things might get ugly. Tommy and I ate Chinese and drank a couple of beers. Around nine fifteen we left the restaurant, and I opened the trailer doors. Tommy grabbed a pile of pads and made himself a cozy little bed. I went up front and climbed into my sleeper. I slept like a newborn babe.

I woke up at seven ready for breakfast and found Tommy sitting on the edge of the trailer reading the sports section of the *Naples Daily News.* His bed was untouched.

Only God and the Devil know what Tommy does at night.

———

Mr. Taylor from Bangor, Maine, was next up for delivery. Ever the meticulous accountant, he had given me a preprinted and completely accurate set of directions. Now that's helping out your mover.

We pulled up at the Taylor house at the stroke of eight. The house was a brand-new Toll Brothers ranch on a golf course. He was very pleased with it. A group of Latino workers were pouring what Mr. Taylor called an Okeechobee porch in the back sunroom by the pool. It was made of smoothed orange and tan Florida pebbles cemented together and evidently a very Naples thing. Mr. Taylor seemed to know all the very Naples things already. He was wearing a pressed pair of khakis and a polo shirt. In the driveway was a brand-new BMW ragtop with Collier County plates they didn't have in Bangor. Mrs. Taylor was wearing a pastel sundress, and the son was splashing in the pool. The Taylors had shed Downeast like a reptile shedding skin. Mr. Taylor explained to me that everything was going into the garage except a few cartons because their Maine stuff didn't really fit with the lifestyle here.

He was right. They'd all do very well here in Naples. I was happy for them. For myself, I was not happy; I kept hauling all this furniture down here for people, and as soon as they saw it in the Florida sunshine, they didn't want it anymore. I could see *their* point . . . it's just that it made what I did absolutely *pointless*.

We finished up the paperwork, and Mr. Taylor signed off on everything. He handed me a fifty and gave me two tens for Tommy. We took off down I-75. I fished out one of the tens from my pocket and handed it to Tommy . . . then I fished out the other one and handed it over. Tommy opened his Cape Codder thermos and poured himself an eye-opener. It was 10 a.m., for crissakes. I watched him cut up his lime and growled at him. I kept the fifty in my pocket. Screw him.

———

Alligator Alley due east from Naples to Fort Lauderdale is one of America's great drives. It's a hundred miles of two-lane blacktop, ruler straight, knifing through the middle of the Everglades. It's a great road going east in the midmorning but a bitch any earlier because the sun is directly in your eyes the whole way. It's the same going west in the late afternoon. You can't see shit. We passed a huge Seminole Indian reservation, massive empty ranches, and lots of signs saying PANTHER CROSSING. This is the final habitat for the remaining dozen or so Florida panthers. Between housing development, Big Ag, and the cars and trucks, I didn't give the panther very long odds. Alligator Alley hasn't got a single strip mall, gas station, theme park, motel, condo, tourist trap, or traffic light. I usually stop somewhere about 50 miles in to feel a bit of the silence and the vastness. I don't linger, though. It's spooky out there. Just a couple of yards from the roadway on either side is the swamp. Sometimes at night, I'll pull over to take a leak and all I can think about is that an eighteen-foot alligator's going to explode out of the water and pull me in. This road is slated to become part of I-75 in a year or two. That will be too bad.

Our penultimate stop was Mr. Warren, going to Galt Ocean Drive in Fort Lauderdale. The neighborhood is called the Galt Ocean Mile and consists of nineteen oceanfront towers highly coveted by those for whom that kind of thing is important. High-rise moving work has its own challenges. I would have to deal with a surly building superintendent, and there'd be lots of rules about when we could work, another set of rules about where we could put the truck, and, of course, loud complaints from the residents about the noise, the truck, use of the elevator, and the overall inconvenience we'd be causing everyone. People always forget that they moved in at some point and caused the same commotion. These high-rises can really mess up the schedule, though; if there was another mover working the building, I'd be dead in the water.

We cruised through the rest of Alligator Alley and met the sprawl at the junction of Route 27. We threaded through twenty-eight miles of the usual Florida thing to the ocean and parked in front of Mr. Warren's high-rise. Unloading in front of me was a United Van Lines truck. The driver had four guys with him, which was a very bad sign because it meant a big move. This was going to take some finesse.

"Hey, United, you going to be here long?"

"Who's asking?"

"Me. I'm the North American behind you. I've got twelve hundred to drop off on the sixteenth floor."

"What time is it now?"

"It's about one thirty."

"I've got thirteen thousand to drop in one little fuckin' elevator. Up on the twenty-second floor I've got two long carries and a shipper who flew in this morning on a broom. I'll be done around five thirty if they let me finish. I hate these fuckin' places. I've already seen the sign. It says: 'No use of freight elevators after 5 p.m.' I don't know if the super's going to enforce that or not."

"Did you ask him?"

"Fuck no."

"How 'bout I buy you and your guys lunch and you let me sneak my twelve hundred in while you're eating?"

"Lunch? What's lunch? Get real, driver. Face the facts. I'm here the rest of the day. Sundays are forbidden, so you're unloading Monday. Go to the beach, go get laid, go enjoy yourself."

"Sounds nice, but I'm loading twenty-one thousand out of Key West on Monday."

"No shit?"

"No shit."

"I wisht it was me, but at least somebody's getting loaded out of this sandpit. God, I hate Florida."

"We have a lot in common. So you'll let me buy you lunch and unload?"

"Not a chance, driver. Your problems aren't my problems."

"How about lunch plus fifty bucks?"

"Nope."

"How about lunch plus a hundred?"

"How about you give me your load out of Key West?"

"So no dice, really?"

"No dice, really. Look, I've got to get back to work. I'd like to help you out, but . . ."

"OK, driver, I understand. See ya."

This was not good. I had told Gary in Fort Wayne my truck was empty. I don't often lie to Gary, but the truth in this case would have cost me my load out of Key West and a six-day net of over $10,000. That's too high a price for the moral high ground. It's one thing to lie to a dispatcher; they know we lie to them just like they lie to us. It's quite another to be caught outright. If I wasn't in Key West with an empty truck on Monday, I might as well go over to Mayflower. Gary would starve me to death. I'd be pulling overflows for months.

I decided to talk to the building superintendent.

"Hi. I'm Driver Murphy from North American—"

"Another mover. So help me God, you guys make my life hell. All you ever want to do is tie up my elevators and piss off my residents."

"Nah, that's not true at all. All we ever want to do is empty the truck and go drink beer. Do you have a note from Mr. Warren about a delivery today?"

The super rummaged through some pigeonholes in his rolltop desk. Clearly this relic was moved from up north and donated to the super by a tycoon's decorator. And for a tax write-off, no doubt.

"Yeah, Mr. Warren. He's away. His note says to let you in today and sign for the delivery. There's a cashier's check here."

"The United guy's got the freight elevator. Can I put pads up on one of the other elevators? There's not much stuff—a few cartons, odds and ends."

"No way. The passenger elevators are off-limits, especially on weekends."

"But United says he won't be done until six o'clock."

"So come back Monday."

"How about tomorrow?"

"Absofuckinglutely not. Never on Sundays. It's etched into the walls around here."

"But Mr. Warren's note says to let me in today."

"So . . . ?"

"You know who Mr. Warren is, don't you?

"I've seen him around. He's not just moving in; this must be some stuff he bought up north."

"That's right. Mr. Warren is the president of the condominium board for this building."

"Rules are rules."

"Sometimes they are. I don't know about you, but I don't want to piss off Mr. Warren. His note says he's expecting this stuff today."

"Can't do it. The tenants'll cut my nuts off, then have me fired, then have me shot, then dumped in the ocean. I'll be shark bait. I've got a wife . . ."

I slid out Mr. Taylor's fifty-dollar bill and laid it gently on the desk.

"Tell you what . . . you let me unload after United over there gets done and Mr. Warren will be happy, and you and your wife and General Grant here will have a nice romantic little threesome at a beach bistro tonight. Your only downside is a couple people bitching about the elevator, but they'll do that regardless of whether Mr. Warren gets his stuff or whether General Grant goes to his final resting place in your Dickies. Whaddyasay?"

"I say I've met the first goddam mover who knows how to motivate people."

"Thanks. I've got to run down to Miami and drop this other little shipment. I'll be back around five."

"I'll be here." I left him rooting through the phone book's restaurant section. I picked up the fifty on my way out. This ain't my first rodeo. An advance payment would have guaranteed me returning to find the whole place locked up with Shark Bait already on the beach slurping his second daiquiri.

We got in the truck and headed south. This delivery was in Kendall southwest of Miami. It was killing me having to drive fifty miles south to Kendall and then fifty miles back to Galt Ocean Drive when I had to drive right past Kendall to get to Key West. But at least my immediate problem of getting empty was solved.

We got back to the Galt Ocean Mile at four thirty, and I went over to check with the United driver.

"How's it going, bedbugger?" I asked him.

"Oh, North American. I didn't expect to see you again. What's up?"

"We thought we'd give you a hand. You know, cooperate. Speed things up a bit."

"You're not unloading here tonight, driver, whatever you do. You're wasting your time."

I was going to enjoy this. "I believe the fix is in for delivery tonight. You have a contrary opinion. It is of no importance. Notwithstanding, Tommy and I are simply waiting around, so I humbly repeat my offer of assistance. We may as well be useful, what? How about I send Tommy upstairs and he can start assembling beds. I'll stay down here and fold some pads."

"Well, I suppose that'd be OK. Thanks. Where you from anyway, England?"

"Indeed not, my friend. I hail from southern Connecticut. Fairfield County, in fact. The Gold Coast it's called, according to some. Others call it Wall Street's bedroom. I call it my heretofore domicile, as my home of late is the humble GMC tractor yonder . . . Enough of this playful banter, sir. So, how do you like your pads folded? Every driver's got a different method . . ."

True to his estimate, United finished at five thirty, and Tommy and I started in on our load. Tommy was wheeling the first batch of cartons into the elevator when the United guy showed up with his four guys. "One good turn deserves another," he said. "C'mon fellas, we can get this done in three trips." We finished Mr. Warren at six thirty.

———

The next morning, Sunday, I missed the eight o'clock breakfast call with Tommy. He came into my motel room at nine thirty looking for me. His bed was still made. We headed south for Key West. I-95 ends in Coral Gables; then it's US 1 from there to the end of the road, literally. Route 1 ends at the Key

West Naval Air Station, where we'd be loading. For once, I could not possibly get lost.

The first time I was in Key West I got bad directions and ended up driving my massive rig down the main drag, Duval Street, just before sunset. I had no idea where I was going and was driving slowly and tentatively. There were a bunch of streamers over the road advertising FANTASY FESTIVAL, and I thought I was going to rip them all down with my trailer. A group of young men were sitting on the rail of a streetside bar saw my plight, and one of them shouted to me, "Hey, driver, do you know where the fuck you're going?"

"No, no idea at all," I replied.

The guy and his friends vaulted the rail and before I knew it six or seven fabulously handsome men in body paint had grabbed the handholds and were standing on my fuel tanks as they rode me through downtown Key West hooting and hollering like they'd commandeered the vessel. Gays, like bikers, have a kinship with truckers. It's probably due to all of us being outside the mainstream. At the turnaround at the bottom of Duval Street the guys told me where to stay, where to eat, and where to go if I wanted company, male or female. It was one of those rarities in my world: an accurate set of directions given by people who actually just wanted to help me out.

Tommy and I got to Key West Sunday evening after cleaning up the trailer at a rest area in Islamorada overlooking the Gulf of Mexico. We parked the truck at the navy base and headed over to the Half Shell Raw Bar for fish sandwiches. We arrived at Helmut's warehouse Monday morning a little before 8. There was an Allied truck there too. I knew Helmut from previous jobs, and there he was in the office, bleary-eyed from the weekend, staring into the distance.

"Hi, Helmut. I'm Driver Murphy from North American. I'm here to load Admiral Clark."

"North American? Clark? That's Allied's shipper."

"Can't be, Helmut. They gave it to me Friday afternoon. Call Fort Wayne."

"I never heard back from Fort Wayne, so when I saw this Allied guy, I gave it to him."

"Where's the phone, Helmut. You're fucking me over here."

I called Gary in Indiana. "Gary? Finn. Helmut here says the job went to Allied, that nobody confirmed my assignment from Friday and he had to reassign it to save his ass."

"Lemme check this, Finn. I'll call you right back."

In the meantime the Allied guy was at the dock loading his trailer with packing material and cartons. My goddam shipment.

The phone rang. Helmut picked it up. I could hear one side of the conversation.

"Aw, c'mon, Gary, you know me. I'd never, ever do that. North American are my number one guys out here. Nobody called me back . . . Yes, I was here . . . No, I didn't leave early . . . The guy's a fucking admiral, he'd have sent a SEAL team to kill me . . . I'm sorry, but I had to do what I had to do . . . OK. You want to talk to your driver?" Helmut handed me the phone.

"Finn. It's Gary. We're fucked. Charlie booked this verbally with Helmut Friday afternoon. Charlie's the boss, and I know he's not lying, but he's out today and we can't confirm it. It doesn't matter anyway. Helmut's really the boss, and he gave it to Allied. The truth is he probably booked it with both of us just to make sure he had a driver. We're on the losing end."

"*We're* on the losing end, Gary? It looks like I'm on the losing end. What are you going to do? First thing I'd say is to delist this fucker from our agency roster."

"That's not going to happen, Finn. He's the only game in town."

"What about me? I just drove two hundred miles to Key West to load a phantom shipment."

"I talked to the planners about that already. We feel really bad about this. I've got seven thousand pounds loading out of Tampa tomorrow for Caribou, Maine, on a GBL paying three grand. There's nothing else on the board, but you're priority one."

"Tampa is four hundred fucking miles from here. Three thousand pays me thirteen hundred to the fucking North Pole. That's a money-losing job."

"That's what I've got. Something else might come in."

My head started pounding and my vision got all blurry. I was thinking about the past eight minutes, eight days, eight months, eight years; the injustice, the slights, the effect on my psyche. I thought about what was happening to me. I thought about the vitriol and cynicism and the bad thoughts coming out of me like bile just on this one trip. I thought again about Lone Ranger up in Kittery. What would he do? What was I going to do? Deadhead up north again to load another snowbird fulfilling *his* American Dream? What about my American Dream? I had a couple hundred grand in the bank.

Every fiber of my being told me it was time to cash in and work on what Lone Ranger already knew. Maybe he had been born that way, or maybe he had gone down his own grueling road of disappointment and failure and figured his way out. The shower at Hal's didn't last long enough for me to uncover the truth. We might have gotten there if I'd put more quarters into my soap. Stephen King once wrote, "Life can change on a dime." In my case, it was a quarter.

"Gary, we've been together for eight years. I want to ask you a question."

"Go ahead."

"How do you look at yourself in the morning? How do you teach your kids ethics? How can you watch me get screwed and spout the company line when you know it's wrong?"

"Between you and me Finn, it's not easy. I've got a mortgage, I've got a family, I've got a job. They've got me by the short hairs. You're a good driver, an upstanding man, but I've no choice except to stand by and watch you get screwed."

"I pity you, Gary. You know what I just figured out about truck drivers? For all their pitiful myths, most of them do this stupid job for one reason: They can look themselves in the eye and honestly say they've held to their own standards without caving in to pressure by society or somebody else's expectations. They might fuck up, and they do, but they own their fuckups and keep to those standards regardless of the personal cost. I'm a truck driver too."

"What are you saying?"

"I'm saying fuck you, Gary. Keep your split-level in Fort Wayne. Raise your kids to become cogs in the machine. I live by a different standard that I just figured out. All these cowboys I've looked down upon—they're better than you, for all their faults."

"Nice speech. Do you want the Tampa load or not?"

"You're not listening, Gary, but I suppose you can't. No. I'm not going to Tampa. I'd leave this fucking rig right here, but I need to do right by Mr. Callahan, so I'll throw away a thousand dollars and park this rig in his yard and hand him the keys."

"You're quitting?"

"I'm just done with this."

"OK then. I've got to reassign this Tampa load."

"Gary, did I ever tell you about the summer I washed dishes at the Howard Johnson's on I-95? The dishes were never done. There was always another rack to load no matter how fast I worked. I was a hamster on a treadmill. Never again."

"Finn, we've had a nice run. I wish you the best, but I've got stuff on my board and my phone is redlining."

"I thought your board was empty, Gary."

"Good-bye, Finn. You were the smartest guy I ever dispatched, but you're not the smartest truck driver. You still don't understand the system. You're not the only guy in the world, you know."

"Oh, I understand the system, Gary, I really do. That's why I'm leaving. I'm the only guy in my world."

"Good luck."

"You too, Gary. You're going to need it more than me."

So that was that. I deadheaded up to Connecticut, dropped the truck in Callahan's yard, and walked away. I had no idea what I was going to do next.

No idea at all.

I quit driving for a long time.

PART III
THE BIG SLAB

Chapter 7
BACK ON THE ROAD

I have a card in my wallet that says I'm qualified to drive any vehicle of any size. It's called a Class A commercial driver's license. Having a Class A CDL is a quasi-mystical benediction, sort of like being a Tolkien Ring-bearer. Like a Ring of Power, it can open up a world of possibility closed to others. It can also bring good or ill upon you depending upon your motivation and luck. A CDL is a lot harder to get nowadays, but once you have one, unless you lose it through some piece of errant stupidity, you get to keep it. Forever.

Even after I quit working for North American, I never considered letting my CDL lapse. I remember joking about it to friends who knew my history, and I'd say, "You never know . . . things might unravel and I might need it again." Well, as it happened, things *did* unravel and I did need it again. Just like Frodo Baggins, when things got too hot, I slipped on the ring of my CDL and disappeared. Long-haul moving is a convenient industry—where else can a man get paid big money for being essentially on the lam?

It was a long time though before the unraveling. I made several U-turns after I left North American, none of them involving truck driving. In 2008 I found myself washed ashore in a city out west where I knew nobody; I was fifty-one years old, single, with no job, no plans, no nothing. I was unmoored. It was the most difficult period of my life. I didn't want to think about how I'd lit the fuse to my previous life and watched it explode. All I wanted to do was to go back on the road. I wanted to climb into a truck, hit that start button, watch the air pressure build up, and go. In that respect I knew I'd have plenty of company among other drivers. That's what we do.

Fifty-one years old is not a propitious age to go back to building tiers in a moving van. I was in decent shape, but moving furniture is young man's work. I wasn't at all sure I could make the grade. What I did know was that I could certainly perform other tasks much better than before. I was no longer a young man in a hurry. I wasn't a young man at all. I was another piece of flotsam hitting the road because I thought I'd run out of options.

Another thing I knew now was that moving, for the shipper, was to experience an emotional nosedive. Maybe I couldn't lift like I used to, but maybe, just maybe, I could use my own failures and hard-earned understanding to grease the wheels of my work and make the experience easier for the people who were moving. Maybe I could breach the wall of suspicion and enmity people have about movers. That felt attractive. I wanted to do it the right way, the way I had never had done it before. I wanted to interact with my shipper and helpers applying compassion and professionalism. I wanted to approach the work itself with serious intellectual intention toward performing even the smallest tasks properly.

With all that in mind, I had the big chat with my old pal Willie Joyce.

Willie had come off the road in 1982 and opened his own moving company, Joyce Van Lines, in Stamford, Connecticut, right after deregulation. Prior to deregulation, interstate moving companies had enjoyed an oligopoly thanks to the Motor Carrier Act of 1935. That act made it nearly impossible for new carriers to enter the industry. Deregulation of the moving industry was started by Jimmy Carter and completed by Ronald Reagan. Any company could now obtain what was called "operating authority" to provide interstate moving services. Moving rates fell by more than half almost overnight. For me personally it was a big financial hit, but it was a far bigger hit for the fat, lazy moving companies with their sweetheart union contracts and bloated management. Those overfed sows were drawn and quartered by nimble, lean, and hungry weasels like Willie. He obtained his operating authority and started taking out the weak zebras in the herd by discounting moves with a fleet of straight trucks. Before long, Willie's workaholism and focus had created a mini van line pulling in $20 million a year. Willie had seven terminals scattered across the United States, a hundred or so trucks, and about thirty long-haul drivers under his broad thumb. The quick-moving, elfin mover with the long hair and goatee I'd known had ballooned into a 350-pound, shaven-headed hydra. He had a fearsome reputation for brooking no bullshit back when he was a driver, and that reputation ballooned like his weight and the size of his enterprise. Picture Marlon Brando as Kurtz in *Apocalypse Now* and you'll have an idea of Willie's appearance and demeanor. Willie ran his company with an iron fist, and had been in the business for so long and was so focused on it that he had a quantum connection with everything. He knew if trailer 169 was missing a stack of pads, and he knew if there was a hedge fund in New Jersey looking for yield that would finance $1.5 million for ten new Peterbilts at 7 percent. And he knew every detail in between. We'd remained friends mostly due to the fact that I'd never worked for him.

That was about to change.

Our chat was about me going on the road for Joyce Van Lines as a driver. Willie was skeptical due to my age and long hiatus. I told him I was going to do it whether he put me on or not. I already knew that I could walk into any of the high-end boutique van lines and get hired on the spot on the basis of my skin color and diction. Guys like me were disappearing because the money was not as good as it once was, while demand for the Great White Mover was getting ever more acute. (High rollers are increasingly impatient with service people they can't communicate with. Industries like moving, landscaping, and housecleaning in today's America are almost entirely non-English-speaking, so I was a highly desirable outlier.) Willie, of course, knew this, so he half-reluctantly leased me a truck.

A few things had changed in the moving business since I was last out there. One was that moving and drinking, and driving and drinking, had disappeared. Another was quality, especially for corporate long-haul operations like Joyce. Now they were rated under a microscope by relocation consolidators like Cartus and Brookfield. If your customer satisfaction metrics didn't measure up, you'd find yourself cut off from corporate moving altogether and back trying to make a living doing local moves. Most of Willie's contretemps with drivers and staff had to do with maintaining the quality standard. If you didn't measure up you were out.

I was pretty sure I'd be up to the job on the quality angle. The way I was looking at moving jobs now compared to before was totally different. I would not be in a hurry, and I would not be obsessed with revenue. The challenge would be to produce satisfied shippers.

Willie leased me an old Freightliner nobody else wanted to drive. To me, after my Astro 95, it looked like a palace. It had a double walk-in sleeper, refrigerator, TV set, and slide-out desk. The cockpit had cruise control, an air ride seat, and GPS. I installed a CD player and a CB radio and bought an AT&T AirCard that gave me internet access anywhere there was a cell signal. I was almost ready for twenty-first-century moving. To reengage my truck-driving chops, I spent a week at a truck-driving school in Denver doing a refresher course. To help me learn the new ropes for high-end executive moving, Willie planned to put me on for a couple of weeks with one of his drivers. That would get me back into the groove.

At the truck-driving school, I picked up right where I left off and deftly performed the parallel parking maneuvers, the backing maneuvers, and the paperwork. Apparently, backing up a truck is like ice-skating and riding a bike. I was doing the one-week course, but there were about fifty guys there doing the month-long CDL course. I could see immediately that trucking hadn't changed at all. Everyone at the school was overweight, undereducated, and looking forward to the big money and free pussy they thought were waiting for them out on the road. When they saw me on the lot doing my turns, they asked me where I'd learned it, and I told them I'd been a bedbugger. That was that. How those guys, without a single paid mile behind the wheel, already knew to ignore the movers was a mystery to me, but I became an immediate pariah. They were all going to the big freighthauling outfits, which seemed to have some sort of hazy relationship with the trucking school that I decided not to be curious about. A couple of guys did ask me about moving work, but when I told them they'd need to load their own trucks and deal with shippers, they lost interest. When I told them a top driver can clear $4,000 a week and more as a bedbugger, they said they were already going to make that once they hooked up with a company. I didn't argue.

The school did a whole morning's lecture on the Interstate Highway System. Here's a kind of fun primer for you four-wheeler drivers out there: On the US Interstate Highway System there's always a mile marker represented by a small green sign on the right shoulder. Truckers call them lollipops or yardsticks. Within each state, mile markers run south to north, so in South Carolina mile marker 1 is one mile from the Georgia border, and mile marker 199 is at the North Carolina border. On a horizontal plane, mile markers run west to east, so on I-80 in Pennsylvania mile marker 311 is at the New Jersey border, and mile marker 1 is near the Ohio border. When truckers communicate with each other, they use lollipops to give a location such as "Kojak with a Kodak 201 sunset," meaning a state trooper has a radar gun at mile marker 201 on the westbound side.

Interstate highways have even numbers for east-west routes and odd numbers for north-south routes. The larger the odd number, the further east it is, and the larger the even number the further north it is. I-5 goes up the West Coast, and I-95 goes up the East Coast. In between, the major routes are I-15, 25, 35, 55, 75, and 85. East-west I-10 (the Dime) goes from Jacksonville, Florida, to Los Angeles (Jayville to Shakeytown). I-90 goes from Boston to Seattle (Beantown to Needle City). In between are I-20, 40, 70, and 80. Three-digit numbers indicate spur routes to the system. Odd-numbered three-digit routes do not reconnect to the main highway; even-numbered routes are circular and are usually beltways around cities. Using Washington, DC (Bullshit City), as an example, I-495 goes around the city, and I-395 ends in the city. It's a simple system that works extremely well except in massive, older urban areas like Chicago (Windy City), where the route numbers coalesce into a Rubik's Cube of confusion.

Every driver should own and use the Rand McNally *Motor*

Carriers' Road Atlas. Get the one with the laminated pages so when you spill your coffee you can wipe it off. It's the best fifty-nine dollars you'll ever spend. Forget about online systems, and don't rely on the voice. It can be useful as a backup, but your primary guide needs to be a map. You need to visualize the route in your mind. Willie Joyce told me that since they started using GPS, drivers get lost or confused three times more than when they used road maps.

———

I was scheduled to meet the Joyce driver who was to train me in new procedures the day after Christmas at the Joyce warehouse in Oxford, Connecticut. The driver showed up late, looked drunk or drugged, and immediately got into an argument with Willie in the office. The discussion heated up, and when the driver came over Willie's desk to make a particularly poignant point, Willie grabbed one of the Bantu spears off his wall (a gift from his sister, a UN aid specialist) and pinned him against a file cabinet with the tip of the spear at his throat. "Call nine-one-one!" Willie shouted. He held him there at spearpoint until the cops came and took the driver away.

Mike, another driver, showed up an hour or so later to load material for a big pack and load in Williamsburg, Virginia, to Las Vegas that would take two trailers. The driver for the second trailer didn't show up (lots of drivers disappear after Christmas), so Willie reassigned me to Mike's load. Willie told me that Mike was a good mover but had anger issues so I should be careful.

Mike was annoyed at being saddled with "a friend of the boss." He made that clear from the moment he refused to shake my hand when we met. Mike's one of those guys who lives out on the road because he can't fit in anywhere else. He was wearing a T-shirt that said MY TWO BEST FRIENDS ARE CHARLIE AND JACK DANIEL'S, which told me just about everything I needed to know. Also traveling south with Mike were two Joyce movers, Nate and Carl. They were to spend the week in Williamsburg packing and loading, and then take the Greyhound back to Connecticut. Neither Nate nor Carl would ride with me in the Freightliner after I told them this would be my first road trip in years. They were sure I'd hit something or slide off the road.

My job was to follow Mike down with the second trailer, help him pack and load, then follow him to Las Vegas to unload. We headed out west on I-84 for the nine-hour slog to Williamsburg. Ironically, at the toll plaza near Newburgh, New York, a four-wheeler changing lanes banged into Mike's trailer. The trailer wasn't hurt, but the four-wheeler was. It took a couple of hours to get all the paperwork done. Mike was sure I had brought black magic to this whole trip. He told Nat and Carl to call me Jonah.

Mike had decided to take the western route to Harrisburg and then south on US 15 to the DC Beltway and down to Williamsburg from I-64 at Richmond. It's not the route I would have picked. It was as if he wanted to test me, a seemingly green driver, to see if I could negotiate the Pennsylvania mountains in the ice and then drive the two-lane US 15 in the dark. But I drove carefully and slowly and arrived in Williamsburg about 5 a.m. I found Mike's truck at the Kmart outside of town, parked next to it, and slept there in my sleeper.

Nate banged on my door the next morning at seven thirty and said it was time to head to the residence. They'd all had breakfast. When I asked Mike if I could grab a coffee and a burrito, he said, "No. If you want to eat, don't oversleep." Words to live by. I could see myself saying the exact same thing to some slacker back in the day when I was the one pissed off at the universe.

We pulled up to the residence of Mr. Bean. He was a big shot in timeshare sales and was being transferred to Las Vegas to clean up the havoc the financial debacle had wreaked. Not a job I would have wanted, to be sure. This being a VIP corporate move, it was our job to pack everything in the house into cartons before loading the two trailers. Mike put me into the kitchen, naturally, as it's the most difficult room to pack and takes the most time. Nate started in on the basement, Carl on the bedrooms upstairs, Mike in the garage. He took the garage because it takes no finesse and he could take breaks in his truck to smoke his Marlboros. The four of us packed nonstop for two days, and I kept right up with them. Packing cartons hadn't changed at all during my hiatus, and I'd been trained in Greenwich, Connecticut, so packing high-value items was a breeze. That didn't stop Mike from coming in periodically and complaining about the small quantity of cartons I had packed. But Nate and Carl kept bringing in difficult items for me to pack and giving me winks in Mike's direction, so I knew I was doing OK. Neither one of them called me Jonah. They called me U-Turn.

Day three was really going to be the test. I wasn't sure if I'd be able to run up and down stairs carrying furniture into the truck for twelve or fourteen hours. Every group of working men has a hierarchy, and I already knew I was number four in this group. Mike was the driver, and the driver is always number one; and though Nate and Carl were pleasant enough, it was easy to see that they considered me beneath them in status and ability.

First up on loading day were Mr. Bean's hickory bedroom sets. Hickory is very heavy wood, and there were five bedrooms, each with a handmade triple dresser, bureau, headboard, and night-stand all built by Grandpa. I had nudged a couple of pieces to check their weight the day before; these were certainly the heaviest pieces I'd ever encountered. We started with the biggest set in the master bedroom. Nate and I padded up the triple and with me going backward we snaked down the curving stairway. I could handle it, just. At the bottom of the stairs Carl was waiting with the dolly to wheel it into the truck. Next came the bureau. and this time it was Carl and me, with me going backward again. Carl was holding the top with a humpstrap, so he had the easy end. When a tall piece like a bureau is being carried down a flight of stairs, it's the bottom guy's job to press the entire weight of the item to clear the top step. I did this one too, with a stop in the middle for a rest. Piece three was the triple from the boy's room. This was slightly smaller than the master but still a serious piece. Nate came up, and with me again on the bottom, we took it down. I was getting a bit shaky, but I was still in the ring. The fourth piece was the boy's bureau. Another monster. Carl grabbed the humpstrap, and we carried it to the top of the staircase for me to press it up. I couldn't do it.

"Carl, I can't lift it. Sorry. Can we switch ends on this one?"

At that moment, Mike came to the bottom of the stairs. "Where's my fucking base?"

Carl, my erstwhile buddy, casually tossed me under the bus, saying to Mike, "U-Turn here says he can't lift it."

Mike ran up the stairs cursing. "I guess I have to hump all the furniture *and* load the truck. Get the fuck out of my way." He pushed me aside, pressed the bureau against Carl's humpstrap, and carried it down and out to the truck.

I was crestfallen. Defeated. I was too old for this work. I grabbed some chowder in my arms and went out to the truck to face the music. Sure enough, there were Mike, Nate, and Carl all standing in the trailer looking at me. I set down the chowder and looked at Mike. "I'm sorry, Mike. I just couldn't lift that last piece."

Mike looked at me and pointed to the pile of chowder. "What

the fuck am I supposed to do with that?" He paused. "You're not very good at math, are you?"

"What do you mean?"

"Well, you guys just took down four pieces. Nate took two and Carl took two, and they were both on the top."

"I don't count who's doing what, if that's your question. I just want to get the work done."

"Well, you won't be worth shit by lunchtime if you take everything. You're not worth shit anyway."

Then Nate started in. "Hooowee, ol' white man!" He was talking to me. "I just made forty bucks on you from cousin Carl here. I owe you one, U-Turn."

"What are you talking about?"

"What am I talking about? We've been looking at you the last two days. We seen you can pack, and we know you're an old fart, and we know folks can pack can't carry shit. I bet Carl ten bucks you'd fade on that first big bastard. When you carried that down, we went double or nothing on the bureau. No way were you ever going to press that muthafucka. When you carried that down, we went double or nothing again on number three. I figured you were for sure going to fade on him, but I was even and had nothing to lose. Carl here's a good guy, but he's got no faith in an old white crystal packer like you. Tell you the truth, I didn't have any faith either, but I for sure wanted to watch. When that third fucker come down, I was impressed and forty bucks ahead. I asked Carl if he wanted to go again, but he declined. You have to respect a man who knows when to quit. I told Mike to come and watch you do the last one, 'cause there's no way any mover can take down four of them monsters in five minutes. When you stopped topside and gave up, I was relieved. No reason for anyone to get hurt here just to please Mike. You an all right mover . . . for a white guy."

Mike broke in. "Nate, are you gonna talk the rest of this shit into the truck or are you going back to work? Everybody, back to work."

———

I felt a lot better after that. The packing had taken two days, and the loading of the two trailers took two more. Two trailers of household goods is not typical even for corporate hotshots. The next part of the plan was for me to follow Mike out to Las Vegas with extra stops in Dallas and Scottsdale. At least I'd get lots of driving practice. I have to say this was a good plan of Willie's to break me back into the business. If Mike hadn't been such an asshole, it would have been perfect.

We left Williamsburg Saturday morning for points west. Nate and Carl both gave me their numbers and asked me to use them for labor when I was in Connecticut. They grabbed the bus and went home. I was supposed to follow Mike, but that unraveled in the first hour. Mike drove very fast, with his longnose Pete and his big Cat engine and his thirty years on the road. He left me in the dust well before Richmond. I called Mike from Spartanburg, South Carolina, in the early evening. He was already at the truck-stop in Atlanta. He told me that when I got there I should stay at a motel he knew nearby that had truck parking and cheap rates.

I pulled into the motel parking lot after dark. It did have truck parking. It also had very dim lighting, and as I walked to the office I saw several women leaning against the second-floor balcony rails yelling greetings to me. I also saw several parked cars idling with men inside. The girls were working girls, and the guys in the cars were pimps. In the office was an Indian guy behind a thick glass partition. I asked him for a room with a trucker's rate, and he asked me how long I wanted the room.

"One night, please," I said.

"The whole night? That will be fifty dollars."

I handed over my credit card, and he said, "Cash only." I carefully forked out a fifty, taking care not to show my wad. There were girls in the lobby too. He handed me a key and showed me where the room was on a map under some Plexiglas on the counter. My room was at the back side of the building at the very end. I asked him if there wasn't a front room near my truck, and he said, "Those are the trucker rate rooms."

I grabbed my bag and walked into the dark. The girls on the balcony were asking me if I wanted a date. I was polite and said I was tired. There were three or four more cars on the back side with engines running. I walked all the way to the end and was just about to insert the key to my room when I saw the curtain move inside. Then I heard a car door slam behind me. I sprinted around the building and back to my truck. Nobody followed me. I drove across to the Days Inn that had a fenced-in yard and stayed there. The next day I called Willie and told him what happened. He laughed. "Mike sent you to that pussy patch? Drivers get killed there."

"I know, Willie. I was about to get rolled. I'm glad you think this is funny."

"Welcome back to the road, laddie. Things don't change much. I'm glad you had the sense to take off."

"Thanks, Willie. Things haven't changed much, and I think your driver is trying to kill me."

"Don't get paranoid, laddie. You've only been out in the wild a couple days."

—

Our first delivery was an extra stop at a mini-storage in Dallas, where Mr. Bean was dropping off one of the bedroom sets.

This load was so full, we we were using the tailgate on Mike's truck—a slideout on the back of a moving trailer that you can load a storage vault on. I met Mike at the mini-storage, and we emptied the vault. Then we had to take the vault off the tailgate, so Mike told me to loosen the straps holding it on until we got to the top one. I did that, and the empty vault was sitting on the tailgate with just one strap holding it. Mike grabbed the ladder and went up high on the driver side to loosen the last strap. I was on the other side, and he called me over. When I moved around to his side, the strap went slack and the vault tipped off the tailgate toward me. Fortunately, the front side of the vault had been taken off to remove the furniture. The vault fell over me, and I was trapped inside. Had the vault still had its fourth wall, I'd have been crushed like a cockroach. These vaults weigh about 600 pounds. Any corner could have caught me too, but I was lucky. I started banging on the sides of the vault and yelling. Mike got a guy from the office, and with a cargo bar they pried the vault over onto its side and let me out.

"What the fuck, Mike? You trying to kill me?"

"I can kill you anytime I want. The strap let loose."

"I don't believe you."

"Believe what you want. Take the clamps off the vault and leave the pieces here. We're going."

We dropped the other stop in Scottsdale and proceeded to Las Vegas. We unloaded Mr. Bean's trailers the first day with a local crew for help, and the next day was to be the unpack day. Mike had locked up the trailer the night before himself. I saw him. On arrival the next morning he tossed me the trailer keys and told me to open the rear doors. Standard procedure when opening a trailer door is to stand a little left of center and open the door a few inches so you can peek inside to see if there are any cartons or furniture against the door. Since we had unloaded yesterday, I knew there was nothing against the door, so I opened it without peeking in. When I did, an eight-foot, 50-pound steel cargo bar crashed down onto the pavement. Had I been looking inside through the crack, as procedure dictated, the bar would have fallen on my head and crushed it like a melon. Someone had leaned the bar against the door just so to make it fall the right way. It was hard to believe it could have been an accident. I'm not sure if I was more frightened or angry.

I went into the house and found Mike. "You missed with the cargo bar, asshole."

"Too bad," he snapped back. "Time is on my side. I won't miss forever."

For some reason I still can't fathom, I didn't leave right then and there. I spent the whole day in the house unpacking cartons. I should have driven away when the cargo bar fell, but I wasn't in my right mind. I distinctly remember going to pieces in Mr. Bean's walk-in closet. I had fallen pretty far. Here I was fearing for my life and working as a day laborer for a nutcase who hated my guts and wanted me dead. I had brought myself to this sorry state without anyone's help through an avalanche of poor decisions. I stayed in that closet for over an hour, carefully hanging up Mr. Bean's Jack Victor suits and crying like a baby.

After the unpack was finished, I told Mike I was leaving and took off. I drove to the Wild Wild West casino, motel, and truck-stop to unwind. I love that place for its easygoing sleaze. I was accosted at the door to the motel office by a young woman who asked if she could borrow my room to take a shower. I told her I didn't have a room and wished her luck. When I came out with my room key, she was sitting in an idling car with a man in the driver's seat. It looked to me like a Mickey and Mallory pair waiting to roll another trucker. The best thing to do out here is keep your head down and mind your own business.

After a shower, I went into the casino to grab a beer and play a few rounds of roulette. When I sat down I looked across at my fellow players, and lo and behold, there was driver Mike, lighting a Marlboro and scowling at the croupier. He hadn't seen me yet. Time to go.

I knew Mike was loading in Salt Lake the day after next, and though I didn't have an assignment, I knew where I was heading: Since Salt Lake is northeast of Vegas, my direction would be southwest. I packed my bag, quit the motel room, and hit the road toward Los Angeles. I was somewhere around Barstow, on the edge of the desert, when the reaction began to take hold. My whole body started shaking, and I had to pull over and let it subside.

My training period was over, and I was still alive. It was time to start reassembling my life. There was no direction to go but up.

Chapter 8
HERE COME
THE MOVERS

Veteran movers never wear jeans. Jeans are too heavy and the heavy sweating that comes with the job causes chafing. Also, jeans have rivets on the seams and require a belt. Either one can scratch furniture or walls as goods are muscled from a home and into or out of a moving van. Jumpsuits of light cotton are preferred because there's nothing to tuck in, nothing to get caught on, and they are loose and comfortable. A veteran mover will also carry his own tool satchel. In it will be his humpstrap, packing tape, a Phillips screwdriver, a flat-head screwdriver, vise grips, pliers, a tube of Elmer's glue, a crescent wrench, a set of Allen wrenches, a bottle of Old English Scratch Cover, a clamp, and a tube of Tibet Almond Stick. With these simple arrangements, a mover can knock down, put together, repair, or hide damage on practically anything to be found in an American household.

I don't bring an attitude or any other expectation on moving day except that the day will be long. I do the best job I can with every move, and I treat everyone the same. Since most of my job satisfaction comes from the work, I don't get too indignant whether I'm treated like a galley slave, a potential threat, an uncomfortable

example of the dark side of the labor pool, or a helpmeet and part-
ner. I try to keep things smooth and easygoing. This is partly selfish,
partly pride, and partly compassion. It's selfish because all of my
workdays are hard days, usually a minimum of twelve hours doing
physical work—and I don't need mental stress on top of that. It's
pride because I know what I'm doing; managing a large move has a
lot of interrelated parts, and all the components need to come
together at the right time. And it's compassion because I understand
that people's identity and security get unhinged by moving.

I've worked long and hard to refine my conduct in order to put
shippers at their ease, and yet after three thousand or so moves, I'm
resigned to the reality that movers are widely viewed as antagonists. I
find this exasperating because I can't figure out why. Our whole
industry can't figure out why. Go to any trade show or meeting of
AMSA (the American Moving & Storage Association) and you'll find
seminars and navel-gazing sessions asking the perpetual question of
the industry: Why does everyone dislike and distrust movers?

We're not so bad. We like to be called by our names and be
shown basic respect. Food and tips are also welcome, but not
required. That's about it. The bottom line is, the movers are in
possession of all your stuff. If stuff is important to you—and it is
disproportionally important to most of the people we move—then
the movers are the most important people in your life for those
couple of days. If we don't get a modicum of respect, well, . . . we
will preserve our dignity one way or another. Shippers don't seem
to grasp that we know more about them in thirty minutes than
their best friends do after thirty years. Movers notice things. Especially the things folks want to keep hidden. We don't carry any
judgment toward mundane bourgeois hypocrisy unless we're
treated like chattel. If we are, we can and often will stir up a shit-
storm. "Excuse me, sir, should I pack this nearly empty vodka

bottle I found behind the laundry soap?" or "Pardon me, ma'am, would you like me to put these gay porn mags into another carton? They were under the tax returns in your husband's office."

Dehumanizing service workers looks to me to be mostly about insecurity. My helpers are almost all Hispanic, and I don't see any profound cultural chasm between an immigrant from Mexico and a middle-class white American. Your standard-issue Mexican or Brazilian is a hardworking Christian who shares a Western historical experience, speaks a Romance language, uses the same alphabet and numbering system, and has similar aspirations. Just because someone doesn't have a grasp of English doesn't mean they don't have a grasp on disparagement. If you think Juanita doesn't know when she's getting slighted, well, she most certainly does know and she most certainly doesn't like it. Rest assured, there's plenty of resentment down here in the service trenches. Alas, only the movers and the cooks have retaliatory measures available immediately to hand.

My default introduction to shippers when they answer the doorbell is to start with a jocular "Here come the movers!" I then smile, introduce myself, and hand over my business card. (Nobody ever gets my name right, so I give it to them in print.) Then I introduce the crew. My crews always have name tags attached to their shirts. (People with names get treated better.) After the introduction my crew will disappear to prepare the trailer and I'll take off my shoes, enter the house, usually into the kitchen, and have a conclave with the shipper. It goes something like this:

"OK. Let's talk a bit about how the day is going to go. When the men are finished outside, we'll prepare the house. We'll cover the floors, walls, carpets, and staircases. That will take about an hour. After that we'll do a walk-through to see what's going and what's staying. Then we'll start packing cartons. Let's use the master bathroom for things you don't want packed, like your clothes, laptops, chargers, modems, cable box, and phones. We'll be here until about six and start again tomorrow at eight, unless that schedule doesn't work for you. If it doesn't, we'll adjust. How does all that sound?"

Usually that will sound fine to the shipper. Then I'll add in some more stuff.

"This is a VIP move being paid for by your company. We want you to be happy with your move. I've got my handpicked A-team here, and I work all the time with these guys. We're not in a hurry. We want it done properly, and properly is what you think is proper."

That's pretty much my opening gambit. What happens in the first five minutes usually establishes the tone on any move. In fact, I only really *know* a move is going well when the shipper disappears. They see us work, they gain confidence that we're professionals, they get bored, and all of a sudden they have to do a few errands, pick up the mail, or meet a friend for lunch. It never ceases to amaze me that these suburban hypersecure control freaks, who have an ADT sign on their lawn, never let a kid out of their sight, and change their garage door code every month, take off after twenty minutes leaving all their stuff under the care of three Latinos and a gray-haired gringo drifter.

I will grant the point that many of my colleagues, while very possibly great movers, might be lacking in certain social lubrication skills. My friend Bill, a longtime Joyce driver, regularly receives negative reviews from shippers. I don't understand why. Bill has the finest trailer setup I've ever seen, with all the right equipment perfectly stowed, custom-designed uniforms, and a full crew who travel with him everywhere. Bill is a tall, lanky man of some kind of color. I think he's half black or half white or a quarter Irish or some other kind of perfectly American mix. Bill is well spoken and generally pleasant, though I wouldn't call him genial. He certainly has that short fuse all road drivers seem to have, but he doesn't take it out on the shipper.

Bill's the real deal way more than I am. He literally lives in his truck and has done so for over thirty years. He has a Direct TV antenna on the roof of his tractor and a generator to keep the rig warm or cool at night. He's redone the tractor interior to house his crew. I was asked to talk to him by Joyce management about his shipper problem when I was flown to Pendleton, Oregon, to finish one of his jobs. The shipper had called the office and told them she didn't want Bill at destination. She said she was afraid of him. I flew into Portland, took a puddle jumper to Pendleton, and met Bill at the Motel 6. We went to dinner at the Waffle House next door, where I buttonholed him.

"Bill, Pete asked me to talk to you about what's going on. Your shipper ratings are uniformly negative, and having to fly me out to drive your truck to residence to complete the move naturally has them concerned."

"I knew this was coming," he said. "Why'd they ask you to talk to me? Can't Pete ask me himself? I've been out here my whole life, and it's nothing personal to you, Finn, but having someone fly in to finish my job is completely humiliating. You and I have always got along fine, but I'm not glad to see you. You're not a better mover than me."

"I know I'm not, Bill. This isn't about you and me or about you and Joyce. It's about you and the shipper. She's terrified of you. She feels threatened. This is a VIP move and we're going to get rated on it. You know the game. We can't have a terrified shipper. As regards Pete, I suppose he figured a driver-to-driver conversation would be better. You and I go back a long time. I'm not a spy for management and I know how things can go wrong with shippers, but this happens all the time with you. Why do you think that is?"

"Honestly, I don't know. I used to think it was a race thing. Maybe the shippers didn't like black guys, though I'm not really a black guy. I don't know what they'd call me. Besides, Perry and

Richard are black, and they get great ratings. So it's not that, though I'd like it to be. Before I got my teeth fixed, I thought that was the problem. But it wasn't." (Bill had been missing his two top front teeth for years. Willie paid to have them fixed up, thinking his menacing mouth was putting off shippers. Whatever people might say about Willie, he's loyal to his longtime drivers.)

"What happened here with this shipper? Any words exchanged? How about your crew?"

"Not a thing. I hardly even talked to the shipper. I did the inventory and loaded the truck. My guys were in and out of the house. To be honest, I'm getting gun-shy about interactions with shippers."

All of a sudden tears sprang into Bill's eyes.

"My whole life's been like this. People just don't take to me. It's like there's this hostility they grab onto when they meet me. Sure, I have a temper when things don't go right, but I'm under control. I've spent my life out here alone on the road mostly because nobody wants to be around me. Why don't you tell me what's wrong with me?"

"My impression is that you do a good job, you're always prepared, always on time, and you want to be liked. I don't get a hostile vibe from you at all."

"So what's wrong with you that you don't get my bad vibe?"

"I've wondered about that. So has Willie, so has Pete. We're all on your side on this. We want to try and figure it out."

"Maybe. They'll probably just fire me and I'll have to go work for Atlas or Mayflower. I like working for a small van line, and I like corporate pack and loads."

"Nobody wants to fire you, Bill. They want to figure out a way to keep you. They know the way you operate, they see you have no damage claims, they see you're totally organized and on the job every day. There's just this thing with the customers. You scare the shit out of them."

The tears sprang up again. "It's not fair. I'm not a horrible person. I overcompensate by keeping my truck perfect, my paperwork pristine, my jobs go smooth, but none of it matters because people don't want me around. I'm a human being. I take up space. I have to be somewhere and I have to work. Now it's looking like I can't even have that because I'm so toxic people have to fly around the country to finish my jobs."

I had no answer to any of that. I just looked at him across the counter.

"You know what else, Finn? I'm not the only guy out here like that. I can't see it in myself, but I can see it out there at the truckstops. I see the guys with the empty eyes. The sociopaths. The crazy drivers holding on to reality with Twinkies, coffee, and Marlboro Blacks that don't have a single thought from one mile to another. They scare me! I never thought I was one of them."

"You're not, Bill. This conversation proves you're not."

"What are you going to tell Pete?"

"I don't know, Bill. I really don't."

"Tell them I'm doing my best."

"They know you are."

"Maybe I should just be a freighthauler and never see anyone from one month to another except forklift drivers and robots. Then I wouldn't scare anybody, but shit, it's such a dumb job. I'm a skilled mover. I can do anything out there that needs to be done."

"You can. Except you don't seem to be able to square away the shippers."

"Yes, except for that. Isn't the rest of it enough?"

"Not when I need to fly to Oregon to finish your job. Perry's not half the mover you are, but you have to admit, he's got charm. Perry has damage on his loads all the time, but shippers don't complain about Perry. You know why? Because they like him."

"Well, nobody likes me."

Bill was right about a lot of things. There *is* a subset of truckers who really are off the mark and choose the job so they can go through life on an anonymous surface paying their bills, keeping on the down low, and thinking or feeling nothing. I had a pretty good idea of what bothered people about Bill. He was an angry man. He was angry about being half white or half black; he was angry that his family had lost the moving company they once owned; and he was angry that he was fifty-nine years old and still a road driver. An angry man, I knew now, since I wasn't one anymore, was a frightened man. I also knew that combining a frightened man with a shipper was a bad combination.

I didn't know how to talk to Bill about this. In our culture, fathers don't even talk to sons about fear so you can be goddam sure truckers don't talk to truckers about it. Bill felt too much and covered up too much. If he could reconcile those to a measured middle, he'd be all right.

———

I had gotten off a long stint of up-and-down West Coast work, which was horrible. I got stuck in some kind of a dispatch vortex where it was San Diego to Seattle, Redlands to Portland, Tacoma to Oakland. As far as I'm concerned, anyone who wants California can have it. The charm is completely lost on me. I finally broke out of the vortex with a load to Fort Collins, Colorado, which is a short jump to my home in Boulder. I was looking forward to some well-deserved time off. At least I thought it was deserved. The Joyce honchos in Connecticut didn't think so, and we had a few words about it. I'm not on the road anywhere near fifty-two weeks a year anymore, and I pick and choose my loads. Part of this is because I get very high customer satisfaction ratings, and part of this is because Willie Joyce is my best friend. Some people in the main office think I'm a prima donna, which is somewhat true, but it's also true that to maintain a high-quality standard you can't burn yourself out on the road.

Willie wanted me to deliver a Mr. Vaughan, who had had to leave his goods in storage near Denver while he found a house. Joyce stored the loaded trailer inside one of their warehouses to avoid double-handling. Our shipper was an electrical engineer for a large aerospace firm. Apparently the company was centralizing its rocket design division and had been moving engineers to Colorado from all over the United States.

I have two Denver-based helpers, Julio and Carlos, both Latinos, with whom I've been working for years. Like Tommy Mahoney in Florida, they only work for road drivers. Unlike Tommy, they hire themselves out as a pair. It's both or none. Julio is in his late thirties and is a single dad. He's tall, muscular, and covered in tattoos. Julio is very polite and well spoken, and he works like a mule. Carlos is short and slim. He's in his early forties but looks twenty-five. He was born in Colorado but has a touch of the sing-song accent you sometimes hear from a native Spanish speaker. This is odd because Carlos speaks no Spanish whatsoever. His grandparents and most of the rest of his sprawling family speak no English, though they've all lived in Colorado for decades. I once asked him how he communicates with his relatives. "It's not easy," he answered. Carlos is a happy-go-lucky guy who always has a smile on his face and a joke on his lips. That's a major asset on a moving van because there can be a lot of tension on the job. Between the shipper, the other laborers, things going wrong, and the difficulty of the work itself, it doesn't take much for things to deteriorate into conflict. Having a class clown like Carlos around keeps things loose.

Carlos and Julio met me at the Sapp Bros. truckstop in Denver to deliver Mr. Vaughan. The trailer came in from the East Coast via a freighthauler. Occasionally, a crew will pack and load a van, and a freighthauler will pick it up and deliver it to one of the Joyce yards for a local crew to deliver. I met the guy early one morning at the yard in Erie, Colorado. His name was Terry. He's not a mover. In fact, he doesn't touch furniture or even open the trailer doors. Terry hauled for a company that moves a lot of our trailers around. Terry was dropping Vaughan and picking up an empty for Los Angeles. I handed him the 20-ounce black coffee I'd picked up on the way over.

"Here you go, Terry. It's a shitty brew, and I didn't know how you liked it, so I played the odds and got it black."

"Thanks. You got it right. Here I am again. Drinking bad coffee before dawn in a dusty truckyard in nowhere, USA."

"How long have you been doing this?"

"Since 1980."

"Me too. I had a good long hiatus in the middle, but now I'm back in the harness."

"I'm so fucking sick of it."

"Did you ever do anything else?"

"I started out hauling green beans in a dry box. Quick turns to grocery warehouses. Then I moved to hauling hay. Now there's a place to exercise some judgement. Do I tarp the load or not? Clear skies and two hundred miles to run. No problem, unless it rains. If it rains, my 80,000-pound load turns into 150,000 pounds, 'cause that hay just sucks up the water. Ever pull into a weigh station weighing 150,000 pounds? They throw you in fuckin' jail. Tarping sucks, but I was in my twenties, right? Jump up and down off the trailer a couple hundred times. Spend a few hours getting it all perfect and it's dry all the way. Decide not to tarp and the fuckin' skies open up. Too much stress."

"What did you do next?"

"Went up to Canada and drove a Terex in a pit mine. That

rig was 150,000 pounds empty, for crissakes. Tires twelve feet high. Biggest goddam thing you ever seen. Scared the shit out of me, driving little mining roads with a thousand-foot drop. I did well there, so they sent me to Chile for six months running a Terex at a copper mine. I finally quit. Maintenance? In a Chilean copper mine? You can say one thing about that job. No logbooks, no pre-trips, no regulations. I just couldn't handle being so scared all the time. The workers hated us, the roads made the Canadian mine look like an interstate, and I was living in a trailer on-site. Nothing to do in the off-time except watch TV in Spanish."

"This is incredible. What else?"

"Eighteen months in Iraq. I made $225,000. That made Chile look like kindergarten. The trucks were locked up every night in cages. Security inspections every couple hours. Pull into a dock with a pit and soldiers crawling up and down and under looking for bombs. I was carrying potable water for the locals. Who'd want to bomb a water truck? Guess what? Every nutcase out there wanted to bomb a water truck."

"What else?"

"Three years frackin' on the Bakken in North Dakota. That really sucked, but I made good money. Lived in an RV the company bought. Four thousand men and twenty women. All whores except for one or two church ladies. Couldn't figure out which was worse. I'm from Christian country in eastern Kentucky. I'm not a Christian, but I'm not a drinker either. Up there you're one or the other. I was neither. That's where I learned computers. I had my laptop and started figuring it all out. I'm very plugged in. It's helped a lot. Plus I read books and listen to books, mostly history. Did you know Abe Lincoln was born in Kentucky?"

"I did. His dad was kind of like you. Kept moving on. The way I remember it, he moved to Indiana and then Illinois."

"Thomas Lincoln never moved to Illinois. He did move to Indiana. Kept buying farms with bad titles. The Lincolns came from the same county I grew up in. White trash, like me."

"I just read a book called *White Trash*. Ever come across it?"

"Yeah. I just listened to it. Heard about it from Terry Gross on *Fresh Air*. Great title. Downloaded it on Audible. I've got an Audible habit that needs a twelve-step program."

"Me too. What did you think of the book?"

"It made me think I'm one of a long line of losers and I'm continuing the line. My son just graduated high school. First one in the family to do that straight up. I've got a GED from a little jail time I did for a domestic way back when. Wasn't my fault, but I figured I'd put the time to good use. The GED qualified me for a work grant to get my CDL, and I used that. I've been on the road ever since. It was my ex who made sure the boy went through school. I wasn't around."

"Does he have any plans?"

"In Paintsville? What the fuck is he going to do in Paintsville, Kentucky? A career choice there is meth or Oxy. Hillbilly heroin."

"How is it going to end?"

"Fuck if I know. He's a grown man. He'll figure it out. Probably he'll get some girl pregnant and the cycle will continue."

"C'mon, Terry, you're a smart man. You've got to have a better answer than that."

My phone rang. It was Pete from dispatch. It was 7:30 a.m. on the East Coast.

"Finn? Pete. You got the driver there?"

"Yup."

"Tell him he's not going to LA. He's going to Connecticut, taking trailer 246."

"OK, Pete." I turned to Terry. "You're going to Connecticut."

"Whatever. I hate the East Coast. Come to think of it, I hate California. I don't care where they send me. Gotta pay my bills. Long as I'm rolling, I'm paying my bills."

"They want the trailer in Oxford by Friday. Do you still have hours?"

"I always have hours. I heard the Feds are going to require electronic logs next year. Did you hear that?"

"That's the story I heard. All interstate drivers will be required to use electronic logs."

"That will kill off what's left of us owner-operators. They'll call it a safety issue, but I'll bet it's the big carriers lobbying the politicians. There was a point somewhere when the big carriers were against government, and then came the point when they figured out they could use government to get what they wanted. I suppose people call that maturity. I call it corruption. As an owner-operator, I'm a dead man walking."

"Me too."

"Thanks for the coffee, dead man. I'll see you in hell, I suppose."

"Hard to say where we're going to end up, Terry. Rubber side down to the coast."

"Sure. What's the fuckin' difference? It's all nowhere. Why are you here, anyway? I could have dropped this off and picked up without you."

"I like to meet the drivers and make sure the transfers are smooth. Between you and me, I like to show a little respect. I bring coffee. I know what it's like out there. It's all I can do."

"Thanks. 'Preciate it."

Terry dropped his trailer and hooked up 246. He pulled away in a glob of diesel smoke and a toot from the air horn. Gone. It's unlikely I'll ever see him again. He was a smart, thoughtful, and defeated man caught in the amber of class, education, and diminished expectations for himself and his progeny.

As a New Englander, from a stable family and a product of a decent school system, I was given a suitcase full of intangible advantages Terry didn't get. Becoming a long-haul driver was, for me, a choice. For Terry, it was the only way out, and he's miles ahead of his contemporaries owning his own truck and making his way. The fact that he seemed to feel no responsibility for helping his son chart his way was mystifying. Where I came from, people fell over themselves trying to grease the wheels for their kids through connections, education, and a certain view of life's potential. Terry didn't bother with any of that. I got the impression he felt defeated from the outset.

I hope that's not true, but it feels true. They say anybody can grow up and be president of the United States, and Lyndon Johnson, Bill Clinton, and Barack Obama are bootstrapping examples that poor folks are supposed to emulate. That's bullshit. Those guys are monumental exceptions used to bolster the myth that anybody can be a success. For every one of them, there are tens of millions of Americans who can see no way out of the pattern. This cuts across race, and it cuts across class. The myth of the trucker as a latter-day cowboy is the same narrative that the urban rapper or the southern rebel adopts to accept his place at the bottom of the American Dream. Terry had no such illusions. He knew there was no way out for him or his son. There's something very wrong about that.

One place you won't find poor whites anymore is on a moving truck. Nowadays most moving is done by Hispanics. It varies by region whether your local mover is from Brazil, Mexico, or El Salvador, but the white guys are long gone and Spanish or Portuguese are lingua franca. This isn't to say that the ownership of the companies themselves have changed because it hasn't. Callahan Bros. is still around, but when that truck pulls up to your house you won't hear any Irish brogues and most likely the only person you'll be able to talk to will be the driver, and even the driver will be chosen for his green card and clean driving record, not his English skills, so you may not even be able to talk to him.

The simple truth is, your latter-day Hispanic laborer, wallowing in the refuse-laden cesspit that constitutes the dregs of the American Dream is more dependable, works harder, and is more trustworthy than many native-born Anglos. The Hispanics actually want out of the cesspit and will work to get themselves out just like the Callahans did a generation or two ago. On the other hand, your typical head-banging, tatted-out, meth freak Anglo doesn't even know where he is. You've pretty much reached the muddy, filth-strewn, windblown end of the American cesspit when you can't find a white guy who can amass the rudimentary requirements needed to be hired as a local mover.

I hear a lot about the immigration problem, but as a guy who works daily in the cesspool, I suspect American business already enjoys the solid immigration policy everyone says we're lacking. American business needs workers to do shitty jobs like humping furniture, and people from poor countries are eager to do these jobs.

———

I was assigned to deliver the trailer Terry had dropped. Per standard procedure, when I got the paperwork, I looked up the address on Google Maps and compared it to my atlas map. Mr. Vaughan had bought a house on a Colorado mountainside. The residence delivery looked so dicey that I decided to drive up there in my car two days before to check it out. A site visit is not typical for movers in general, but I'm a careful guy who doesn't like surprises, and besides, I like to perform top service for our corporate clients. The Vaughans' house was certainly going to be what we call a shuttle, which is when I have to bring a smaller truck and transfer the goods into that because there's no tractor-trailer access. The residence was two miles from any pavement, and his "street" was a 10-percent-grade gravel track with several twists and turns that on my best day I couldn't negotiate with a trailer. Even if I could, it was a dead end at the top.

I'd scoped out a turnout about three miles down from the residence where I could park the trailer. I'd also transferred the first load onto a straight truck at our yard so we could start unloading into the house on Monday morning. Carlos and Julio had worked the day before, a Sunday, to get it all ready. I parked the big truck at the turnout and took over the straight truck from Carlos. Even in a straight truck this grade was gnarly, and it was drizzling rain, making the dirt road gooey. If the truck was going over the side, I didn't want Carlos behind the wheel. I got stuck going up the first grade because I was hesitant at the hairpin turns and slowed down too much. I had to back down and start over. I had the guys go up ahead to block traffic so I could keep my momentum. I got the truck in low gear and was redlining the tachometer at 3,500 on the flattish first section. As I climbed, the tach slowly dropped to 2,500, then to 2,000, then to 1,500, and I was lugging the engine. It just didn't have any more juice. I realized I shouldn't have loaded the thing full. Just before the truck gave it up and stalled, I hit a flatter section. My guys ran up ahead to stop traffic at the next group of hairpins. I picked up my rpm to 3,000 and dealt with the next grade. We did this three times before I backed into the Vaughan driveway at 7:59 a.m. We were greeted by Mr. Vaughan and an iPhone on a tripod, filming us.

"You were supposed to be here yesterday," he said.

"Hi, Mr. Vaughan. I'm Finn Murphy from Joyce Van Lines. Here's my card. I was assigned by the office to deliver today. I'm sorry if there was some confusion. This is Carlos and Julio. We're here to make this move as smooth as possible."

"That's not the truck my stuff was loaded into. My stuff was loaded onto a trailer. I took down the number. It was trailer 248."

"Yes it was. Trailer 248 is just down the road. We had to transfer your belongings into a smaller truck to make the hill. It's called a shuttle."

"Why wasn't I informed there was going to be a shuttle? I don't want my stuff to be double-handled. It makes for more damage. I was told it was going to stay on the trailer."

"Mr. Vaughan, you're an engineer, right?"

"I certainly am."

"Well sir, as an engineer, can you tell me how we can get a tractor-trailer anywhere near this house?"

"You can't. Still, I should have been informed."

"Maybe so. If there's any blame, it's me. I drove up here on Saturday. I've been driving trucks since 1976. If there was ever a reason for a shuttle, this is it. We barely got the straight truck up here."

"I was wondering about that too."

"Well sir, we're here. Ready to start. We're going to prep the house and get things rolling."

Our plan was to unload into the garage and then move items into the house. Mrs. Vaughan was sitting on a lawn chair attending to the tripod, taking video of the unload with a notebook and pencil on her lap. The first item off the truck was a pushbroom. I asked her where she wanted it to go.

"That broom is dirty. Somebody used it. It was new back in Pennsylvania."

This was probably true. As I've mentioned before, movers do not covet other people's stuff, with one exception—a pushbroom. All moving vans need a pushbroom because the hardwood trailer floor gets filthy with the residue of people's faulty housekeeping. You move out a refrigerator or a barbecue grill and all of a sudden there's a dusty, filthy mess on the trailer floor. It's dangerous and ugly, and I like a clean trailer. John Callahan told me forty years ago that a "clean truck is a happy truck," and he was right. I'm a stickler on the point. The problem with brooms is that the truck's broom often gets delivered to the residence by mistake. (Nobody ever files claims on items delivered that don't belong to them, which are most often brooms and extension ladders.) This pretty much always leaves a driver looking for a broom. I don't deliberately steal brooms, but I often end up with one that's not mine. In this case, the origin driver most likely used Mrs. Vaughan's broom to sweep out the dust, trash, ashes, coins, dust bunnies, mouse turds, and bits of food left behind from her own house.

"Yes, Mrs. Vaughan, this broom has certainly been used."

"I'm going to write it up as damaged."

"You're certainly entitled to do that." She started writing in her notebook. This was not going to be a smooth couple of days. One of the advantages of moving work is that I have very limited time with problem people. I'll be with a shipper three days a week at most. I pity, up to a point, the postal worker who is consigned to a hostile work environment for two or three decades. It must be hell.

We took everything off the truck in pads and unpadded most of the items in the garage. The overstuffed furniture, big bedroom pieces, dining room table and chairs, and the usual good stuff people have, we unpadded inside the house. Mrs. Vaughan ran from room to room taking video of the unpadding and scribbling into her notebook. It all looked fine to me, but she was writing frantically. After we finished the first load, we went down to the trailer to load the second shipment. Mr. Vaughan came with us and shot video of the transfer. More notes. By 5 p.m. we had unloaded the second shuttle and there was a half load left in the trailer. We told the Vaughans we'd load the last shipment onto the straight truck and finish the next day. This time Mr. Vaughan didn't come to do video. It had started to rain again. We loaded the last half load onto the straight truck, and I took the trailer back to Erie and left the straight truck at the turnoff.

When I got home I had a message from Mr. Vaughan. They had gone out to have dinner, but on the return home their four-wheel-drive vehicle had gotten stuck on the hill due to the mud caused by the rain. Mr. Vaughan's message said he was wondering if we'd be able to get the truck up the hill in the morning. That was helpful.

The next day we picked up the straight truck at 7:30 a.m. Pouring rain. I took the wheel and started up the hill like the previous day, but it didn't work because the road had turned from gooey to gumbo. At the first grade my wheels spun in the mud and the truck started sliding backward down the hill. I got really lucky and managed to keep the thing out of the ditches until we hit the flatter grade at the bottom. This was the point where the smart money stops and waits for the rain to end and the road to dry. But I've never been a fan of the smart money, and I knew Mr. Vaughan would be working the phones if he had to wait a few more days. I didn't want that. From the perspective of the company paying for the move and my own office, there are only two phone calls wanted: one to say I'm there on time and unloading, and one to say I'm finished and the shipper is happy. Any other call for any other reason is driver ineptitude.

I called Pete in operations and asked for approval to hire a tow truck to drag me up. He gave me a curt no and hung up. My next option was to try backing up the hill to the house. I knew that the reverse gear had slightly better torque than the lowest forward gear and that the weight on the rear tires might get better purchase. Also, if I was going to slide downhill again, I figured it was marginally better to be facing forward.

Julio and Carlos manned the turns again, and I backed the truck up the grade. It worked, but it took a long time. We arrived at the house at 9 a.m. Carlos and Julio were soaking wet from the two-mile walk in the rain, and I was soaking wet from fear and stress. Mr. Vaughan came out holding a Venti Caramel Macchiato.

"You're late."

"It was a challenge getting up the hill."

"We expected you at eight."

"Yes. We'll make up the time."

"You can't make up time. That's nonsense. What do you know about time? When it's passed you can't get it back."

"I know a little bit about time, sir. It's time to unload."

The Vaughans spent the day doing more video and criticizing all of our work. They filed a damage claim a few weeks later for over twenty grand. I'll cop to a ding on their dining room table . . . and the dirt on the broom. Other than that the claim was bogus. But the van line paid it. I was debited my deductible of $1,600.

———

Just when a jaundiced view of humanity was about to infect my soul with cynicism and resentment, fate dealt me the opposite hand to mess yet again with my worldview. The contrasts I regularly deal with would be so much more fun if I could just learn to roll with them more effectively. I'm getting better, but obviously, the challenge is rolling with the hard ones. The easy ones are similar in that the shipper accepts the instant intimacy, and our shared humanity is acknowledged. When that happens we can actually have a relationship, short-lived as it might be, but no less authentic for that.

That's when this came through:

Shipper Dewan Bronx New York to Colorado City Arizona
22,000 lbs 2,416 miles Line haul $21,000 Pack and load COD
Extra stop at origin.

It was a full load paying over twenty grand, plus a full pack worth maybe five grand. Packing Monday/Tuesday, loading Wednesday, unloading Monday. That's a one-week turn grossing fifteen grand, of which I'd pocket ten after expenses. Ten thousand a week has a nice ring to it.

I arrived at the Dewan residence in the heart of the Bronx at 8 a.m. after an early start from Oxford, Connecticut. The Dewan house was in the middle of a teeming block of identical working-class row houses. Fortunately I'd only brought a small pack van for the day's packing. I was going to have to call the New York City traffic department and get the cars off the street for Wednesday's loading day. My 53-foot trailer would completely block the road if I stayed out on the street. Also I was going to have to hire an extra guy to sit in the truck. In neighborhoods like this you can't just let an open moving van sit there. It would be stripped in five minutes. (I learned this the hard way in Boston when I was unloading on Commonwealth Avenue, in a decent neighborhood, and a guy ran up the walkboard, grabbed a bicycle off the tier, and rode away. I was standing on the ladder inside the truck at the time and watched the whole thing happen. The sheer nerve was astounding. By the time I'd gotten over my shock and went to chase him he was long gone. So now I have a guy who just stays on the truck looking mean. It works but it's expensive. (What I need is a scarecrow that looks like a mover.)

I walked up the stoop steps to the metal-barred storm door and rang the doorbell. It was answered by a small, middle-aged Bengali man.

"Good morning, Dr. Dewan. My name is Finn Murphy from Joyce Van Lines. I'm your driver. Here's my card. This is Tommy and Jeff. We'll be helping you move over the next few days."

He beamed at us with owlish eyes. "Good morning, Finn and Tommy and Jeff. My name is Nobel. Please come in and meet my family. This is my wife Ranya and my infant son Rafik. We are all very pleased to meet you. This is a great day in our lives. We've been working toward this for ten years. We are all happy to meet you and have you share in our joy. Will you have some coffee? We serve real Arabian coffee in this house. I think you will like it."

"Why, thank you, Doctor. I think we will join you. We can go over some details then as well."

"Most excellent! Thank you. Ranya? Coffee, please. Please sit down, all of you. Let's have a chat."

Now there's a nice way to greet your movers. Arabian coffee in the living room with a charming man who remembered all our names. Ranya brought in the coffee on a tray with a pot, cups, and saucers and served each of us with a shy smile, asking if we wanted cream and sugar. I felt like I was having high tea at the Plaza.

After pouring, Ranya disappeared, and Dr. Dewan started in.

"Let me tell you why we're so happy to see you. I was born in

Bangladesh and received my MBBS in Dhaka. It's a good medical degree but different from the American one. I moved here ten years ago and spent five years driving a taxi while qualifying for my American MD in obstetrics. For the past five years I've had a private practice here in the Bronx. We've done well here, but it's too crowded and noisy. Compared to Dhaka, of course, the Bronx is like an open meadow, but it's still too much. We always wanted to live out west. We saved our money, worked hard, and now we're off. I think you have the extra stop listed on your paperwork? The extra stop is my office. We'll be moving all my medical equipment from there also."

"That's a great success story, Doctor. Congratulations," I replied. "I'm happy for you and your family. How did you come to pick Arizona?"

"Thank you, Finn. I can see you are happy for us, and that makes me happy too. I picked Arizona because my job is to deliver babies. Lots of babies. The more babies the better. I'm good at it. When we started seriously thinking about moving, we looked for places with lots of babies being born without a lot of doctors. It came down to Amish country or Mormon country. We picked the Mormons."

"Why is that?"

"Because most of the Amish live in Pennsylvania, Ohio, and Indiana. There are pockets everywhere. Sarasota, Florida, has a population; so does Wyoming. But I needed a larger community, and I wanted to be out west."

"What are the Mormons going to think about a Muslim doctor from Bangladesh delivering their babies?"

"I wondered about that too. I went out there several times and spoke to people in Colorado City about that very issue. Everyone was thrilled. There are not enough doctors out there, especially ob-gyns, and they have lots of babies. Have you ever spent any time with Mormons?"

"I've moved lots of Mormons. Corporate America loves them."

"Do you have a general opinion about them?"

"I have. Every Mormon family I've moved has been pleasant and low-keyed. We're always fed and treated nicely. On the other hand, they have lots of stuff. Tons of food in the basement, toys everywhere, and multiple bedrooms for all the kids."

"Pleasant and low-keyed. Exactly. We'll be fine. I bought a beautiful house out there for less than this row house here. Eight bedrooms on ten acres. I'm going to be a cowboy. More coffee?"

"No thanks. We need to get to work. This has been very nice. Thanks again."

We spent the day packing cartons. I was intrigued by this situation in a couple of ways. First, 22,000 pounds is a lot of stuff for a family with one kid. That mystery was solved when we went into the basement. It was all medical equipment. Examining tables, file cabinets, machines, scales, boxes full of gloves, bandages, everything. The good doctor must have been haunting medical-supply yard sales for years. The other thing was their courage and determination. My own family came from Ireland, and they moved into the Irish ghetto in New York and went to the Irish churches and hung around with other Irish. Coming to America was probably a challenge, but they kept to their social networks, so the culture shock had to have been somewhat muted. These folks were from a far different cultural mileu than any Irish peasant and going it alone out in the Wild West. Reminds me of some of the Chinese. You can go into the furthest reaches of, say, Montana or northwest Ontario and find some little dusty town with a hitching post and a church, and there will be the Chinese restaurant. Inside will be a family with the man in the kitchen, the wife serving tables, and the kids doing homework 500 miles from the next-nearest Chinese person. It takes brass balls to do that. I couldn't, for sure.

We worked until five, and I took the pack van to my mother's house in Connecticut. My mom cooked me a steak, and after dinner I looked up Colorado City, Arizona. It was a Mormon town, all right. In fact, it's ground zero for the plural marriage set. The doc was right; lots of babies. I woke up in the middle of the night, and that's when the penny dropped. I couldn't wait to talk to Nobel the next day.

We started day two with coffee again. Ranya had diffidently asked us not to pack the coffee set until the very end. There we were, in the living room, sitting on the sofa, and I put it to the doc straight up. "Say, Dr. Dewan, I looked up Colorado City last night. You're right, they have lots of babies there. Apparently the reason for that is that lots of the guys out there have lots of wives. I suppose you knew that."

"Yes, I knew that." A smile began pushing at the corners of his mouth.

"And you bought a house with eight bedrooms for you and Ranya and Rafik?"

"I did." His smile was getting broader.

"I'll be damned. You're planning on starting a little dynasty out there, aren't you? When do your wives start coming in from Dhaka?"

"I've no idea what you're talking about." He was beaming at me. "Do you disapprove?"

"I have no dog in the hunt one way or another. I'm just amazed at the brilliance and audacity of the plan."

"Yes. It will work. We will hide in plain sight among the FLDS. They really are thrilled about us coming because they do need doctors. They're patient people. They probably envision a bunch of brown Mormons in a generation or two. That could happen. Of course, Muslims can be patient people too. *Inshallah*."

I started laughing. Ranya blushed. Dr. Dewan turned his face back to me, grinning from ear to ear, pinning me with those sparkling, merry eyes.

"More coffee, Finn?"

Chapter 9
INVISIBLE MEN

My first year back on the road was mostly a fun adventure. For the first month I had my nephew with me, which helped a lot. He had been a mover during his college days and was between jobs. My first load was a nice one for Bechtel Corp. out of Tampa for Hanford, Washington. Bechtel had received a $10 *billion* contract to stop a plume of radioactive groundwater from reaching the Columbia River. My shipper was an engineer on the project. From Hanford, I picked up another full load in Seattle for Los Angeles. I'd gotten my mountain-driving chops back after successfully navigating Deadman Pass (aka Cabbage) into Pendleton, Oregon, Snoqualmie Pass into Seattle, and Tejon Pass (Grapevine) into Los Angeles. I'm more comfortable with mountain driving these days, but I've no desire to drive in the ice and snow ever again.

Mountain driving isn't difficult exactly. If you're calm and willing to go slow, it's reasonably safe. The problem for me is that while I'm going 25 mph down a 6 percent grade I have a lot of leisure to think about what could go wrong and then imagine ensuing repercussions. It comes down to what you're used to. I know guys that will scoff at Vail Pass but turn into burbling babies at the thought of New York. My first day driving a tractor trailer had me over the Third Avenue Bridge into Manhattan and it hardly fazed me. Of course I was a very young idiot at the time. I still drive into Manhattan, and I'm always respectful, but it doesn't freeze me like it would some driver from Wyoming who'll do a 10-mile 6 percent while singing Willie Nelson on his CB, talking to his girlfriend on his hands-free, and heating up a burrito in his microwave.

I got a General Electric exec back to Fairfield, Connecticut. The pace was calmer than the North American days, or maybe I was more relaxed. I kept my logbook strictly legal, hired lots of help for my shipments, and stayed in motels almost every night. All I was doing was VIP pack and loads, and the emphasis was totally on customer service and not quick turns. That suited me just fine. The money was amazing, and my account at Joyce Van Lines swelled nicely in spite of the expenses. It costs me about $25,000 a month to operate full-time out on the road. The lion's share of that is labor and fuel.

I picked up an ex-investment banker with his $3 million worth of loot going to Aspen. My regulars, Julio and Carlos, and another helper I use regularly, named Eduardo, drove out from Denver, so I had my A-team crew. My shipper, after helping topple his bank in 2008, caught another plum job with another troubled public company that was paying for this move. Without getting all Eugene Debs about it, it seems to me that while many bad movers end up in orange vests picking up trash on roadsides, many bad executives get new million-dollar jobs running other companies into the courtroom.

I rolled into Aspen and parked at the Bavarian Motel. I had called previously to ask if they could accommodate my truck, and the desk clerk said he'd arrange it. He also told me the trucker rate was $149 a night, a huge bargain for Aspen. I booked one room for me and one for the lumpers. When I pulled up next to the motel I saw a hundred-foot row of orange road cones the desk clerk had put out to save the spaces for me. I was snug on South Mill Street in downtown Aspen with a tractor-trailer right across the street from the Grand Hyatt. Unbelievable.

The boys met me in the lobby about 8 p.m., and we ordered a pizza. They asked to talk to the delivery guy in person, saying that they had to give him directions. They negotiated a pickup of a twelve-pack of Coronas with him and sat by the pool smoking cigarettes until he arrived. I grabbed a slice and a Corona and went to my room to fill out my logbook and go to sleep.

At 7 a.m. we headed out to the residence. We got through the security gate, found the shipper's house, and prepared to unload. I knocked on the door, which was answered by a middle-aged Latina. She let me in and led me through the entryway into one of the living rooms, across the art gallery, and into the chef's kitchen with the stainless Sub-Zero and the granite island (each stone no doubt manually shaped by Lake Como virgins using nail files). Fifty grand worth of copper pots that could have served lunch for the Army of the Potomac hung on hooks above the island. I won't go into any further detail about what amenities a $25 million starter castle in Aspen has, except to mention the eight bedrooms, the eleven bathrooms, and the Olympic-size pool in the basement. It was an older house, maybe almost a decade old, so it was regrettably missing some key necessities for a twenty-first-century 1-percenter, i.e., the home theater, the wine cellar, and the Sonos Bluetooth sound system. I stood there at the kitchen entrance for a few moments and watched my shipper in a deep huddle with a woman and another man. The shipper was a short man with graying auburn hair, about forty-five years old. The woman, his new wife, was a statuesque blonde about thirty, and the other guy, the builder, was a tall slim man wearing a starched shirt with French cuffs. They were talking wine cellars. I stood there a while longer and then emitted a delicate Jeeves-like cough to announce my presence. The shipper, let's call him Mr. Big, looked over at me and said to the builder guy, "I'll be right back. I need to deal with this."

Mr. Big ambled over. I introduced myself, gave him my radiant road-driver smile, handed him my card, put out my hand to shake, and said we were here to move his stuff in.

"OK," he said, ignoring my hand. "I'm kind of busy. Consuelo can tell you where everything goes. Do you need anything from me?"

"No sir. It will take us a bit of time to prep the house. We'll cover the white carpets and pad the walls. Is there anything you need from me?"

"I don't think so. How long do you think you'll be here?"

"Well sir, there's quite a bit of stuff and a lot of uncrating. We'll be here until five or so."

"That long? Can't you move faster?"

"I've got my best crew in from Denver, sir. We won't waste time, but we do like to do things properly, and properly will take us to five o'clock."

"Fine. Deal with Consuelo. By the way, if you'll be here all day, will your guys need to use a bathroom?"

"Probably, sir. The normal procedure is to designate a guest or staff bathroom for the crew. We have our own cleaning supplies, and we'll make sure it's shipshape before we leave."

"Well, that's not going to work. You see, my wife—"

"Sir, I have three handpicked men and myself. We do VIP

corporate moves all the time. We'll be respectful, but we are required to answer the call of nature."

"Can't you go down to the security shed?"

"Well, I suppose we could, but that would mean moving the truck two miles each time. That will take the job into tomorrow."

"Tell you what. Across the street they're putting in my tennis court. They have a portapotty there. Use that."

"Yes sir, we'll use that."

"OK then. We're done here." He turned away to talk wine cellars, tennis courts, and home theater.

We prepped the house and started unloading. In addition to a bunch of cartons and some rolled rugs, there were twenty-five crates holding eight 600-pound pieces of granite and seventeen art canvases. For VIP moves like this, we're authorized to uncrate everything and set it where it's supposed to go. We'll do everything except hang pictures on the wall.

We finished unloading around noon. We worked fine with Consuelo; she spoke no English, but both Julio and Eduardo speak Spanish. Eduardo grew up in Longmont, Colorado, but spent five years as a pimp in Juarez.

At noontime, the shipper's threesome disappeared. They returned an hour later with a bunch of bags from the deli downtown and proceeded to set up luncheon at the granite island. I eased into the kitchen to tell Mr. Big we'd completed unloading and would take a short break before commencing the uncrating. He took a long bite out of his hoagie and said, "Fine." I looked at all the food bags, sort of waiting. We don't expect to be fed by our shippers, but when the nearest deli is thirty minutes downvalley and I had spent twenty minutes backing my rig down the winding driveway, it would have been thoughtful to ask the movers if they wanted anything from town. Not Mr. Big. There would be no

luncheon provided for the proles. I went back to the truck and told
the boys we'd be skipping lunch. Eduardo looked at me and said,
"Maybe it's time to throw your white around."

"Throw my weight around?"

"Throw your *white* around. You never heard that term before?"

"Meaning what exactly, Eduardo?"

"Meaning we're brown guys and you're the white guy. To
throw your white around means you're supposed fix the situation
with your palefaced amigo."

"I've never heard the term 'throw your white around,' but I like
it. Problem is, I'm not white enough to throw anything around
with this guy. We're already pissing in the portapotty, we're already
starving. Do you think this guy looks at me any different than
you?"

"I guess he doesn't. How do you like being a brown guy?"

Just then Carlos came into the truck. He looked at me and
winked. "Let's get this fucker done. I'll start unpacking boxes.
Julio, hand me your knife." Julio put up his hands. No knife.
"Eduardo, let me borrow your knife." Eduardo shrugged. No
knife. "How about that?" said Carlos. "Three Mexicans and no
knife." Everyone laughed, and the tension was broken. Carlos figured that since we'd have the Bavarian Motel for another night
we'd hit Aspen later and gorge ourselves. He told me his cousin
said we needed to go to the Hickory House for ribs and order the
two-person, $72 "Feast" from the menu. Carlos said that if we
added a bucket of Modelo's to the rib platter, it might go a long
way toward dealing with the day. I told him that sounded like an
excellent plan. Carlos smiled and became the happiest man on
earth as he humped the crates while his tummy was rumbling,
knowing that a feast at the Hickory was going to end his day. I
envied his attitude. The nice thing about hard work is that it even-

tually ends. When it ends, there's a hot shower, sore muscles, and, if you're lucky, a few cold Modelos and a pile of ribs. That's enough for Carlos, and very often enough for me. Eduardo, on the other hand, hadn't yet finished his personal Occupy movement. "I asked you a question," he said. "How do you like being a brown guy?"

"I'm OK with it mostly, Eduardo. If I let it get to me, then I'd be pissed off like you. The shipper doesn't know me, or you, and he doesn't care to. It's not really about us. We're just pieces of the machine to get his art uncrated."

"Well, it pisses me off. He's treating us like dirt, and you can't change it. There's going to come a time when I'm going to get really pissed off at both of those things."

"Your problem, Eduardo, is that you can't stand being a mover. You think you're cut out for better things. You've got a certain dignity that you're not able to release. You're in the wrong business. Look at Carlos, he doesn't let this stuff bother him."

"Carlos is an idiot. At least when I was a pimp I could keep my dignity."

"Carlos looks brilliant to me. He takes what he's given and smiles through it all. I wish I could be that smart. So you were a dignified pimp? Look at what you had to do with your girls. You could keep your dignity, but they couldn't keep theirs."

"They didn't have any."

"You sound just like our shipper. Do you think he's better off being on top of the pile and you're worse off being at the bottom? What is it you want? I think you want to be over there discussing wine cellars and treating the rest of us like dirt."

"You're exactly right. That should be me over there."

"Remind me never to move you when your ship comes in, Eduardo. How about we get this job done and go eat some ribs and drink some beer?"

"That's enough for Carlos. Maybe even for you. Not for me. You're just playing at this shit anyway. Mr. Great White Mover with a house in Boulder, slumming with the brown guys for some kicks. That pisses me off too. I should kick your ass."

"It's not that much of a game humping furniture and being treated like I'm invisible. I do the same work as you, and I drive, and I do the paperwork. Ever read *Invisible Man* by Ralph Ellison?"

"I'm not much of a reader."

"Too bad. You'd like it, but it would piss you off even more."

"I don't need that."

"No, you don't. Still, it can be a comfort to know you're not the only one annoyed at the status quo."

"I couldn't care less who else out there is getting disrespected. I only care about me getting disrespected. You like this work. I fucking hate it."

"Eduardo, my doing this has nothing to do with you. But you're right, I do like it."

"If it was all you had, you'd hate it."

"There might be some truth to that. Let's finish this and eat some ribs."

"You can't buy me off like Carlos with some fucking ribs."

"I'm not trying to buy you off. I'm simply asking you to enjoy the ribs with me and Julio and Carlos. If you want to kick my ass afterwards, fine. It won't change your circumstances and it won't quell your anger."

"Maybe afterward I won't be so angry."

"Do you really think that?"

"No. But I really do think I need to release all this anger at somebody."

"I've got an idea. How about we fuck the shipper?"

"How?"

"Leave that to me. I'll get him where it hurts. Right smack in the center of that bloated ego of his. I promise you it will be good."

"That might get me through the day, but I still want to hurt somebody. I'm going to tell Consuelo that this house is famous for a murder and that it's haunted. If she's the kind of Latina I think she is, she'll be gone by five. Maybe we should invite her for ribs."

"Let's go back to work."

Julio and Carlos missed this little existential conversation. They were working. They had definitely not missed the scene at the kitchen island with all the food, though. They're more used to this than I am. Brown guys in Colorado don't get a lot of respect. On the other hand, they could have shopped yesterday for today's lunch instead of drinking beer at the motel pool. But that would have taken foresight, which none of my guys have in abundance. For my part, I generally don't eat at all when I'm working, so I didn't think of their lunch. Well, I'm not their babysitter.

We attacked the crates. The eight granite pieces we wheeled in were gravestones from Chinese emperors. Mr. Big told us to be careful, since each one cost $85,000. He had eight pedestals custom built in his gallery to showcase them.

Before I dropped out of my chic northeastern liberal arts college, I took Chinese for one semester. I was there just long enough to learn some rudimentary characters. I knew that Chinese reads from right to left, and I knew the vertical orientation. I was damned sure Mr. Big didn't know Chinese from Pig Latin, so I had the boys set up the slabs upside down. Sooner or later Mr. Big would have a cocktail party and be bragging about his pilfered gravestones to somebody who knew Chinese. He didn't care about the movers, but he would care about being exposed as an ignorant Philistine when it was pointed out he doesn't know up from down on his six hundred grand worth of stolen rock. It wasn't a big victory, but down there on the moving trucks, it was enough.

We finished the job. No tip, naturally.

After showers at the motel, we took a cab to Hickory's and ordered two "Feasts." That's when I told them about the gravestones. They all laughed their asses off. Even Eduardo.

Just as we were leaving, Consuelo came in with her husband and three kids. Eduardo had told her the gringo driver would buy her family dinner. Eduardo knew I would, of course. I shook hands with Mr. Consuelo, nodded at the children, and left my credit card number with the hostess. I don't know any Spanish, but when I was walking out the door to the taxi, a little bit buzzed on six or nine Modelos, I saw Consuelo cross herself several times in front of Eduardo. On the way home Eduardo told us Consuelo had quit. She told him she knew there was something wrong with the house, and the occupants, but hadn't figured it out until Eduardo told her about the murder.

Chapter 10
BABY GRAND

"Finn, I've got a good one. Wanna to hear it?" It was Pete Ruggles on the phone. Pete runs long-haul operations for Joyce Van Lines and is an industry lifer. In a weird irony, he also went to Colby College, and graduated, so we have that old college bond. We call each other from time to time just to chat or pass on a crazy moving story.

The afternoon of this call I was peeling off Ben Franklins into the eager palms of Carlos and Julio, having just delivered another rocket scientist to Colorado.

"Sure, Pete. I always want to hear strange moving stories. What happened this time?"

"My old pal Nick from Bingo Movers in New Jersey just called me. Seems their driver was supposed to deliver six thousand pounds plus a baby grand to residence this morning. I don't know what happened, but the driver unloaded the stuff onto the shipper's driveway and took off. The piano's still sitting there on its side in the sunshine with the rest of the shipment."

"Jeez, Pete. Must have been a really bad shipper. What'd he do? Ask the driver for his green card? Rap sheet? Tell him this is

America so speak English? Maybe he looked on the sex offender website and saw his driver's picture?"

"Dunno. All I know is the whole load is still in the shipper's driveway."

"Sounds bad. Good thing it's not your problem. Not mine either. We're going to lunch at Miner's Tavern. It's Philly cheese-steak day."

"Well, Nick asked me if I could help him out. He's an old buddy, so I'm going to try. When something this bad happens, it's appropriate to circle the wagons and show some solidarity."

"I couldn't agree more, Pete. You're a good guy that way."

"Yeah. I'm going to have to send a crew to clean it up. You'll never guess where this guy's driveway is."

"Oh no, Pete! Fuhgeddaboudit. I thought this was a social call. Stupid me. Not nobody, not nohow."

"Afraid so, Mr. Wizard. It's fifty-five miles from where you're standing. Evergreen, Colorado. Looks like it's going to rain too."

"I'm going to make you say it, Pete. What is it you want?"

"I want you and your crew to go up to Evergreen and take care of it."

"When?"

"Now. Actually, sooner than now. Nick said money's no object."

"You want me to take my trailer out to Evergreen with my boys, finish the unload, including a baby grand, calm down this crazy shipper, make everybody happy, and money's no object?"

"Yup."

"When a mover's in trouble, charge them double. I'll do it for two."

"Two what?"

"Thousand."

"That's robbery, Finn. Nick won't go for it."

"No problem, Pete. Tell Nick to work his Rolodex while I eat my cheesesteak. You're right, it is going to rain. Something to do with the cumulonimbus formations. I'm not really up on the science, but it rains in the mountains every afternoon about one forty-five in the summer. I hope the shipper signed off at sixty cents a pound. If he bought replacement coverage, Nick's in for an Olympic-size claim. Those baby grands don't like to take baths. Screws up the soundboard for openers, and those little felt thingies inside are like sponges; they just soak up the water. Plus, I hear the metal strings rust up real quick—"

"Stop already. The shipper's got full replacement value at seventy-five thousand. Ralph's deductible is twenty thousand."

"Oh well. Too bad for Ralphie. Two grand sounds like a steal. In fact, it's too cheap."

"Enough! What's the cut for Joyce out of your two grand?"

"How about zeeerrrooo, Pete. Nick is your buddy, and this is off the books. I'll bet Willie doesn't even know you're calling me."

"What are you going to pay your guys out of that?"

"I think this conversation is getting off track. I'm enjoying it, though. I never, ever, get to dictate terms, so I'm really going to milk this. Am I going for a cheesesteak or going to Evergreen?"

"Have the shipper sign a paper that says Joyce has *no* responsibility on this. Do that before you touch anything."

"Sounds like we're doing the deal."

"We're doing the deal. Go fix it."

"I'll do my best, Pete."

This was interesting. I asked Carlos and Julio if they wanted lunch or three hundred each to work the rest of the day. They were suspicious. I explained the situation, and they opted for the three hundred. So out of the two thousand, I'd pocket fourteen hundred after paying the boys while using the Joyce truck and the Joyce fuel. That's not bad by any standard, but there were uncertainties. The shipper was bound to be somewhat disconcerted, and, this being Colorado, we might be greeted at gunpoint, or by a posse of close friends in an ugly mood. Regardless, we were ready. I fired up the tractor, hooked up an equipment-loaded trailer, and headed out to Evergreen.

The exurbs west of Denver are mottled with winding roads sporting thousands of homes built into the mountainsides. Towns like Conifer, Genesee, and Aspen Park sprout up practically overnight, and developers grab any piece of ground that can hold a foundation to build somebody's dream house in the hills. It's a zoning nightmare and typical of Colorado. When easterners think of Colorado, they think of pristine mountain vistas and John Denver. Colorado, in fact, has more in common with southeast Florida, Phoenix, and Los Angeles when it comes to land use. The primary goal is to get the politicians to provide as much publicly subsidized infrastructure as possible so the real estate honchos can build more houses, condos, strip malls, and blacktop. The secondary goal is to have the existing taxpayers pay for the new schools, sewer plants, roads, and police departments that these same taxpayers didn't ask for. People always seem to be puzzled when their bucolic communites get overrun by sprawl. Well, guess what? It didn't just happen. It was planned, years before, by the developers and the elected officials in the town hall. Even more likely is that the developers *were* the elected officials in the town hall. Most people are too busy changing diapers and getting the kids to dance recitals to notice what is really going on out there. You can trace the entire arc of American history back to real estate scams starting with the Colonial Ordinance of 1648 in Massachusetts, which is still in effect. It's actually even earlier if you want to dig a little. The pilgrims in

Plymouth and the second and third sons of English gentry in Jamestown may have been starving to death, but that didn't stop them from platting all the ground. Our elementary school history books say that George Washington started out as a land surveyor. Well, he was sort of a surveyor. What he really was was a real estate speculator on a grand scale, as were most of our founding fathers.

Here's an interesting historical question: Why did so many American Civil War battles take place near courthouses? We've got Spotsylvania, Amelia, Jacinto, Stafford, Dinwiddie, and Appomattox, to name just six. Why were there so many courthouses in the rural USA in the nineteenth century? Was there so much theft? No. Robbery? No. Crimes of violence? No. The reason was that everybody was suing everyone else over land possession, ownership, titles, and development rights. Well, the real estate interests settled it all down over the ensuing century by operating quietly and effectively so that the path of unbridled development looked like progress and the ensuing sprawl looked random. It may have been progress, depending upon your definition, but it certainly wasn't random. As a result we have all these swaths of low-density sprawl all over the country.

Evergreen is one of these. Miles and miles of roads and scattered houses where school bus rides are mini road trips and you have to drive half an hour to get a pint of milk. I was climbing uphill in the truck around the hairpin turns when I saw what looked to be a large yard sale. This had to be it. I parked on the main road before negotiating the driveway. This was potential hostile territory. If I was the shipper I'd be supremely pissed off and panting to take it out on somebody. Julio was in the lead with his 240 pounds and six feet three inches; Carlos was next, his taut frame expressing menace. I was last in line, looking for a rifle barrel sticking out a window. There wasn't a sound. It was a little past

1 p.m. as we passed through the mess in the driveway, veered around the piano lying on the pavement, and rang the front doorbell. I heard a baby crying, then footsteps, then the door opened, and there was our shipper, Mr. McNally, a pleasant-looking young man, holding an infant. Mrs. McNally was behind him with a toddler on her hip. I bravely stepped in front of my phalanx.

"Mr. McNally? I'm Finn Murphy from Joyce Van Lines. I'm here to make things right."

"Thank God," said Mrs. McNally.

"I've no idea what happened here and don't need to know, but a short summary might be useful. Can you tell me anything?"

"Sure," said Mr. McNally, "The driver showed up this morning and started to unload with his crew. We were in here with the kids. All of a sudden the truck left with everything still in the driveway. I called the office in New Jersey, and they said they'd figure it out. That's all I know."

"You didn't have any words or anything with the driver or the crew?"

"Nothing. They came in, said hello, everything seemed fine, and then they were gone."

"Well, I'm very sorry about all this. We're a local crew. This is Julio and Carlos. We'll get this all sorted out for you."

"That sounds great."

"There will be no more problems. Let's do a walk-through and see where everything's going."

The residence was what they call an upside-down house, which meant the kitchen and living room were on the second level and the bedrooms on the ground level. They're built that way so the mountain vista, really just a view of other houses and power lines, is enjoyed from the living level. On the ground floor there was a small interior stairway with a sharp turn leading up, and an outside stairway leading to a deck and the entrance to the kitchen. The house was built in the 1970s and was a total piece of shit.

I was thinking solely about how we were going to get that baby grand lying in the driveway into the house.

I've always enjoyed moving pianos. Piano moving has that magical combination of specialized knowledge, finesse, and bull-dog determination that appeals so much to my personality. In fact, I like moving them so much I'm going to give you a sketch of how to move a baby grand. First off, when the piano is sitting in your living room, it's on three legs with the pedal assembly below, a cover above, and a music stand above the keyboard. There are very few doorways that can accommodate the girth, so the piano is moved around on its side. First I take off the cover, which is on hinges. I lay the cover on several moving pads, cover the top with more pads, and then tape the whole thing perfectly so no wood is showing. Next I unscrew the hinges, remove the pedal assembly, and pad all of that. All of the hardware goes into a plastic bag, which is tied to one of the legs. Next I slide out the music stand and pad that. Now comes the harder part. To get the piano onto its side, I first take off the leg at the bass end of the keyboard. Each leg is attached by a metal flange, which goes up and then in to lock it into place. Most legs come off by taking the weight off the leg and tapping the top section inward to release the locking interface. I do this by taping a moving pad to the leg and then a piece of wood to the pad. While my two movers take the weight off the leg, I tap the wood with a rubber mallet, and the leg releases. The two movers gently lay the corner of the piano down onto a long padded piano board. Now one corner is on the piano board and the other two legs are still attached. Next, we lift the entire piano onto its side, and the other two legs are sticking out horizontally. These get taped off and padded, and now the entire piano is on the piano board. We pad the piano and tape it to the board and then attach two heavy-duty straps to grooves in the side of the board and tighten the piano onto the board. It's relatively stable there but I always have a guy holding it to maintain balance. Next, I attach a humpstrap to the front of the board, and two men lift the front end while I set a four-wheel piano dolly underneath. Now we can roll the piano on the dolly. This is all pretty straightforward, and pianos aren't hard to move, provided you can wheel it to where it needs to go. You can even lift it over a step or two with the dolly. The difficulty starts when it needs to go up or down a set of stairs. You can't use the dolly. The only thing that works is brute force.

The McNallys' piano was not going up the interior stairway because of the narrow turn. The outside stairway had fourteen steps with a straight shot through the kitchen into the living room, so that was the only viable route. There was no walkway to the stairs, just grass. My plan was to lay plywood from the driveway to the bottom of the outside stairway. Since we were moving this in, not out, I'd put the piano on the board in the driveway (the previous movers took their piano board with them), put it on the four-wheel dolly, and wheel the piano to the bottom of the walk-board, which sat on step seven.

That all worked out fine, and we wheeled the piano up the walkboard with Julio on the front humpstrap pulling and Carlos on the bottom pushing. (I was standing next to it, holding the balance.) We pushed/pulled one step at a time until it got clear of the walkboard and dolly and was flush along steps seven through eleven. Now we had 600 pounds of piano, wood on wood, at a 45-degree angle. I couldn't push or pull because I had to hold the vertical balance. With Carlos on the bottom and Julio at the top, they tried to muscle the thing up the incline. No dice. Basically we were short one strong man. I took a second look at the stairway. It was attached at the top by two galvanized joist hangers. I didn't like the look of that at all and started doing the math. There's me at 200 pounds, Carlos at 150, Julio at 240, and the piano at 600. That's a shade under 1,200 pounds being held by two joist hangers. It was holding now, but the real test would be when the full weight of the piano got to stair fourteen and the two joist hangers would be holding the whole thing. It was time to stop and think.

First of all, I didn't want anyone getting hurt. If the stairway gave way, we could all get very hurt or very killed. Second, this move was already a mess, with a much-distressed and unhappy family. Third, we were hired to execute. Fourth, we had to be in Laramie, Wyoming, the next day to load another shipment.

Here were my options:

1. I could get another mover out here to help push. I rejected this because adding another 200 pounds to the staircase looked even more dangerous, given the flimsy construction, and anyway, I didn't have another mover available.
2. I could have told Mr. McNally the stairs didn't look safe and he could contact a rigging company to hoist the piano. I rejected this because the McNallys were at the end of their rope, and I didn't want to cause them even more stress. Also, I figured this was my problem, and I didn't want to give up.
3. I could attach straps to the piano board, string the straps over the far railing of the deck, attach the straps to a vehicle, and have the vehicle pull the piano up the stairs, with Carlos and Julio holding the vertical balance with ropes on either side away from the staircase.

I took Mr. McNally outside and explained the options to him. He told me the piano was his wife's treasured possession and he really wanted it in the house. He thought option 3 was the most practical and said we could use his Jeep. That's when I brought out the release form and he signed it.

We set everything up. I was in the Jeep with the cargo straps attached to the piano board, and Carlos and Julio were on the vertical balance ropes. I put the car into gear, tightened up the slack on the straps, and began pulling. It worked perfectly. The piano moved easily up the incline, and the tip came over the top step. But just when all the weight was on the joists at the keyboard end, they gave way with a groan and the stairway fell apart. The piano did a back flip, pulled the jeep backward, and dropped ten feet onto the ground with a final chord just like the one at the end of *Sgt. Pepper's*. Julio and Carlos dropped their ropes and ran. I'll remember that sound to my dying day. Like a whale groaning in its final flurry, the baby grand sang its death song.

It got very quiet for what seemed a long time. Mr. McNally was standing some distance away with the infant and just stared. Mrs. McNally came out with the toddler and joined her husband. Carlos and Julio came over to where I was standing after stopping the Jeep. I looked over at the family and saw silent tears running down Mrs. McNally's face. Mr. McNally put his arm around his wife's shaking shoulders and started crying too. Then the kids joined in. We just stood there, silent, watching this nice young family take the punches. They hadn't wanted to move to Colorado. He'd lost his job in New Jersey, and his in-laws who lived down the road had rented this wreck of a house out in the sticks for them to start over in. The move had gone over the estimate, the driver had abandoned them, and the A-team cleanup crew had just destroyed their most beloved possession. Julio was wiping his eyes; Carlos the Mexican bandit was bawling out loud. So was I. Julio went over and put his arm around Mrs. McNally's other shoulder, and she put her arm around his. Then Carlos went over, and then me. There we were, a bunch of broken people with nothing left but our shared humanity and grief and loss and failure. There wasn't anything left over for anger or blame or apology.

I don't know how long we stayed there, but then the thunder cracked and the skies opened up for the afternoon rainstorm. At first there were only a couple of drops, and then came the deluge. Mrs. McNally looked over at the driveway, where all their stuff was still lying around where the driver had left it. The pads and boxes and furniture were all getting soaked. She stared at the pile for several moments and started to laugh. She looked at her husband and murmured, "I guess we keep on going, right?" Mr. McNally set his kid down and opened his arms to the rain and started laughing too. "Bring it on!" he shouted. Julio yanked off his shirt, put it on the infant's head, and ran to load what he could into the garage.

I walked over to the truck, took the soggy release form from my pocket, and laid it carefully on the seat so it wouldn't get ruined. I felt like a total shit doing that.

The storm lasted only a few minutes and passed away. The remnants of the piano were still attached to the board, and we wheeled it into the garage. We brought everything else into the house, assembled the beds, and unpacked all the cartons. We stayed very late putting everything where it belonged, setting up the kitchen, and putting away the linens. We all wanted the house to look like a home before we left, but there was no ignoring the gaping hole in the living room where the piano was supposed to go. There wasn't a lot of chat. Finally, when there was nothing left to do, we put the wet pads into the truck and went into the house to say good-bye. Mr. McNally was sitting at the kitchen counter with his checkbook.

"What's the bill for you guys today?"

"There is no bill. Nick in New Jersey said it's all covered."

"That makes sense. Here, take this and split with your men."
He handed me a hundred-dollar bill.

"I'm sorry, we're not taking that."

"There were plenty of mistakes made today all around. You guys worked hard. Please take it."

"Not a chance."

"Do you think I can file a claim for the piano?"

"You'll have to talk to Nick about that. We were never here."

"The phantom movers. In and out like the fog, never to reappear."

"Pretty much. We tried to help you, and we tried to help Nick. All we did was make everything worse."

"Believe it or not, everything was worse before you got here. After the piano went overboard and we got rained on, everything got a little better. It's hard to explain."

"I guess we all got banged on the head about what's important and what isn't." I said. "Someday this is going to become one of those family legends you tell around the Thanksgiving table."

We drove back to Erie in silence. Julio went to sleep in the sleeper, and Carlos just stared at the road. At the yard I parked the truck. Carlos took off in his car, and Julio woke up.

"Shit. Where's my shirt?" He was only wearing his sleeveless undershirt.

"You left it with the kid."

"Damn. That means we were there after all. I thought it was all a bad dream."

"It was both, Julio. See you at five a.m. We're off to Wyoming."

Chapter 11
WAITING TIME

I knew I shouldn't have stayed in Nebraska. I should have driven over to Denver and waited there for a General Electric or Verizon move. Instead I've got a military:

Shipper Howard 13500lbs GBL pack & load OA Omaha Line haul $12700 DA Anaconda Movers Brighton MI.

We call them GBLs for Government Bill of Lading. GBL moves are charged on a contract rate that the government negotiates with the big haulers and they're all cut-rate moves. There's very little money in hauling them, but there is something to be made on the packing. This one I've got is a GBL pack-and-load going to Michigan.

It's not great but not horrible. At least I'll get the packing. Military moves are different in that *everything* gets packed into a carton. I don't often think about who's moving where, especially for military people, but Lakeland, Michigan, seemed an odd place to send a lieutenant colonel of infantry. Still, I didn't worry about it. I've moved lots of military folks over the years and though most them go where you'd expect—North Carolina, San

Diego, Texas—there's a lot of weird stuff going on in the post-9/11 world, and the armed forces have facilities everywhere.

The Howards lived inside Offutt Air Force Base. On-base housing is often a problem for movers because the security folks at the entry gates perform background checks on everyone coming in. Anyone trying to get on base with a felony record is turned away. This reduces the pool of available movers by about two-thirds. The Howard residence was your general-issue, senior-officer ranch house. I arrived with my crew at 8 a.m. and Colonel Howard met us at the door in full uniform. He was five feet seven inches tall with muscles that bulged out of his uniform. He shook my hand, very firmly.

"I don't like moving and I don't like movers. I've moved a lot. I think you're a bunch of undisciplined vagabonds. If you've got a problem with that, I'll take off my uniform out back and we can argue the point with our fists."

This was odd. Our shipper wanted to beat us up, and we hadn't even broken anything yet. I spoke for myself and, I assumed, the crew:

"We're fine with that, Colonel. I *am* kind of an undisciplined vagabond. We're just here to do our job."

"I have work to do at the office. It's just up the road. Call me if you have any questions. My wife will be here but do not bother her. I'll handle all the details. Any questions?"

"No, sir," I answered. I wanted to salute.

"Then go do your job."

We started in packing cartons. Mrs. Howard spent the day sitting at the kitchen table chain-smoking, silently watching us pack her belongings. She was a ghost. There was a kid too, an awkward teenaged boy named Trevor who played with his electronic game thingy all day in his room. Neither one of them said a word. We packed the house the first day and loaded the second day. I was scheduled to unload three days later and only had 700 miles to travel so I didn't have any time pressure.

I picked up Interstate 80 in Council Bluffs and spent the night at the Iowa 80 truckstop in Walcott. It claims to be the largest truckstop in the world and even has an antique truck museum on-site. Iowa has lots of truckstops, which means lots of competition, which means they still have actual restaurants. Most truckstops have gotten rid of their restaurants. Trucker staples like chipped beef on toast (also known as shit on a shingle), the iceberg lettuce salad bar, and the all-day breakfast menu are no longer available nationwide. Maybe that's not the greatest loss to civilization, but did they have to replace every restaurant with a Subway franchise? The floor of my truck is usually carpeted with that Subway shredded lettuce product. You can't smell it, you can't taste it, but you can sure as hell spill it.

——

The next day I picked up I-94 west and stopped for the night in Ann Arbor. In college towns—like Chapel Hill, Boulder, Iowa City, Missoula, Austin, Madison, and Oxford, Mississippi, to name a few—all of a sudden, instead of unemployment, meth labs, and poverty, there are real jobs. Plus you can get a latte and a pack of American Spirit Golds. Municipal officials always seem to want auto assembly plants and call centers, but a real and lasting economic engine gets running when there's a university in town. As far as I can figure, the only places left in America that can boast of vibrant downtowns are college towns and high-end tourist towns. In the rest of the country the downtowns were hollowed out when nobody was looking. You might think it's only your town that's been ruined by sprawl, but it's happened everywhere.

You've got the new CVS, the Walmart, the Home Depot on the fringes, while the old downtown is either empty or the buildings have a Goodwill store, an immigration law office, and an "antiques" store, meaning junk. The chains on the outskirts provide the nine-dollar-an-hour jobs and wire the day's receipts to Bentonville or New York every night.

I hate it personally, but we deserved what we got. We wanted the eight-dollar sneakers and the forty-five-cent tube socks. Well, it's not unlikely that those socks and shoes were made by a twelve-year-old girl in Madagascar more or less chained to a machine. While we were happily buying goods on the cheap, the developers were buying the local politicos on the cheap and getting the zoning changed so they could build even more big boxes. We didn't consider that maybe it'd be a better bargain to pay twenty dollars for sneakers and buy them from the neighbor who owns the shoe store downtown and stocks sneakers made in Maine.

It's too late now. The game's been won by companies who don't give two shits about community character or decent jobs. Congratufuckinglations, America! We did the deal. Now we've got an unlimited supply of cheap commodities and unhealthy food and crumbling downtowns, no sense of place, and a permanent underclass. Yay. This underclass isn't relegated to urban ghettoes either. It's coast to coast and especially in between. Take US 50 west from Kansas City to Sacramento or US 6 from Chicago to California and you'll see a couple thousand miles of corn, soybeans, and terminally ill small towns. It looks like an episode from *The Walking Dead*. If there's such a thing as the American heartland, it has a stake through it. What's left are factory farms and meatpacking plants far off the main roads jammed to the rafters with immigrant laborers getting paid who knows what.

So let's all enjoy the cheap pork chops while wearing our new sneakers, because we paid a heavy price for them.

This country has almost twenty thousand towns, and I'll bet I've been in or through most of them. The pattern of sprawl on the fringes and decay in the center is firmly established everywhere. The other thing, just as firmly established, is American mythmaking. I love seeing tourist posters of America the Beautiful. In New England the cultural icon is the small town with a white church, in the West it's the false-front frame saddlery with the hitching post, in the South it's the roadside peach stand, and in the Midwest it's a ruggedly handsome farmer in a John Deere hat. Oh really? Is that what America looks like? I'm all over the country all the time and guess what? There are barely any family farms left in the Midwest, hardly anyone goes to church in New England, the Georgia peach groves are tract houses, and towns in the West are either bedroom communities or ghost towns. If a tourist poster of America were made with some verisimilitude, it would show a Subway franchise inside a convenience-store gas station with an underpaid immigrant mopping the floor and a street person at the traffic light holding a cardboard sign that reads ANYTHING HELPS.

———

Central Michigan north of Ann Arbor was more of what I was just talking about. I arrived in Lakeland the night before I was scheduled to unload the Howard family. The Colonel had picked out the house on a day trip the month before. It was a decrepit farm dwelling outside of town, all by itself on a little rise. It was a lonely, windy spot. I had a couple local guys with me and we went in. Mrs. Howard looked upset. This being a military job I was required to get clearance for delivery from the transportation officer (TO) at the air force base in Nebraska. When I called in, the TO told me to hold off unloading. He said there were issues that might take a couple days to resolve but that I was authorized to receive waiting time. Waiting time is great because it pays something like $450 a day and all I have to do is hang around. I went to talk to Mrs. Howard.

"I'm not authorized to unload today. Do you know what's going on?"

She gave me a rueful smile. She was pretty in a wounded sort of way. I guessed she was in her mid-thirties.

"Yes, I know what's going on. I'm refusing to move here. My husband picked this place out. I haven't heard from him since we left Nebraska, and the last conversation we had was that his job transfer probably wouldn't happen for a while, so he'd be staying on base during the week and try to come to Michigan on the weekends, or some weekends."

"What's his job out here? This doesn't look like army territory."

"It isn't army territory. All his work is online. He can work anywhere."

"You must have family here, or he does. I suppose it could be a nice place to live . . . if you knew some people or had some connections."

"Nobody's from here and we don't know anyone. It's penance."

"I know a lot about penance. You must have committed a pretty big sin to be given all this." I indicated the house with the peeling paint and the brownish hills.

"My sin was that I wasn't what he expected. My bigger sin was that our boy Trevor wasn't what he expected either."

"I know a lot about sin too. Unfulfilled expectations doesn't fit the definition. *A sin is a grievous offense, done with sufficient reflec-*

tion, with the full consent of the will. That's Irish catechism class, verbatim, circa 1965."

"It sounds like you're offering me absolution."

"Not at all. Absolution requires a sin and penance requires a transgression. It doesn't look to me like there's been either one. This looks like punishment. This is like dumping Napoleon on St. Helena."

"At least Napoleon got to bring a few friends along, and St. Helena had ocean views. That's what's got everyone running around in circles. An army wife is supposed to obey. They're confused. So am I. I've been married for sixteen years, and I've always done what I'm told. I'm not a tough person. My mom was a military wife too, so I thought I knew the score. But my husband is a block of granite."

"How does it feel to be laying your line in the sand?"

"Amazing. For the first time in my life the people in charge are wondering about what *I* might want. It's fun."

"Congratulations on your first nose-thumbing at authority. It *is* fun. I've built my life around the concept. It can also be dangerous."

"Dangerous for whom? I might decide to just do whatever the hell I want from now on and to hell with the Colonel and the US Army and everything, except Trevor. It looks dangerous for them."

"Now you're talking. The TO has me on waiting time. He said it might take a couple of days. They're going to try and convince you to stay here."

"Good luck to them. Everyone's scrambling down at the base trying to figure out what to do with the crazy wife. Do you think I'm crazy?"

"Not at all. I think you were maybe a little crazy in Nebraska. Now it looks like you're getting a little sane."

"Me too. What does a mover do on waiting time stuck in the middle of nowhere?"

"Not much. I'll find out if there's anything interesting around and check it out. I'll get a motel room in town. I've got a barbecue grill in my truck, and I like to make my own meals at night. I read a lot. This kind of thing actually doesn't happen very often, so it's a nice break. Besides, Uncle Sam is being very munificent. I think they'll lose patience with this whole deal in a day or two if you hold firm. What will you do in the meantime?"

"The realtor said there's a nice lake up the road with a swimming dock and picnic area. I'm looking at this like Trevor and I are on summer vacation. If you can find the lake later, come on by. I'll give you the latest breaking news from the army about the crazy wife."

I had no answer for that. I paid off my crew, dropped the trailer in the driveway, and bobtailed to the local motel.

The clerk was polite but curious as to what I was doing in Lakeland. I told her just enough, and she told me if I was on waiting time with nothing to do I should go to the lake because it had a swimming dock and picnic area. There wasn't anything else to do or anywhere to go.

———

That afternoon, I drove up to the lake in my tractor. Sure enough, there were Mrs. Howard and Trevor under a picnic canopy. The lake was a lovely spot and practically deserted, this being a weekday afternoon.

They looked pleased to see me. Mrs. Howard smiled at my approach. "You came to the lake after all."

"It's a highly recommended place. Your realtor and my motel clerk both gave the place high ratings."

"That truck looks funny," said Trevor. "Like a midget."

"I know it does. When there's no trailer connected, it's called a bobtail. Wanna see the inside?"

"Nope."

"No interest at all? That's un-American. I thought every kid wanted to see the inside of a big truck."

"Not me, and I'm not a kid. I'm fifteen."

"Sorry. How's the water?"

"Cold."

"You're just a bundle of sunshine."

"This place sucks."

At that point Mrs. Howard jumped in: "I'd like to see the truck."

"Really?"

"Yes."

"OK." I was glad I had cleaned it up. After a few travel days the interior can get pretty raw. Nothing horrible, but there will be empty coffee cups, fast-food wrappers, full ashtrays, Gatorade bottle chamber pots, and dirty bed linens that can coalesce into a distinctive aroma unnoticeable by the primary occupant. I unlocked the passenger side and helped Mrs. Howard climb up the monkey bars into the cab. She sat in the shotgun seat and looked around. "You sleep back there?"

"All the time."

"It's so cramped."

"Not as cramped as my last truck. This is a palace, believe it or not. But yes, it gets tight. That's why I'm at the motel in town. I can spread out a little."

"That's the opposite of my experience. I live in a big house with a cramped life. You live in a cramped house with a life that looks big and exciting."

"A lot of people think that about truckers' lives. If my life is big, then a lot of other lives are microscopic."

"You don't see it because you're in it. Many other people's lives *are* microscopic. Mine is, or was. You have to understand that my husband's plan was to exile Trevor and me out here. He was never going to come. He wasn't going to divorce me or anything. That would have hurt his career. He was just going to live on base, and with a bit of luck and time we'd just dissolve. Kind of like putting an unruly dog out to a farm family. You tell yourself the dog got a good home and then you forget about it."

"It sounds like this has been going on a long time. What prompted the move now?"

"Trevor."

"How?"

"He just turned fifteen. He doesn't want to see your truck. He doesn't play *Grand Theft Auto* and he doesn't want to shoot guns, hunt ducks, or do calisthenics."

"I see."

"Yes."

"Pretty tough on the Colonel, eh? He didn't get the playmate he wanted."

"He didn't get the wife he wanted either, but that's just how it is. Reality is at odds with his idea of what should be. Rather than adjust his views, he finds it simpler to remove the impediments. And they're calling *me* crazy?"

"I think I understand."

She stood up, leaned over the doghouse, and kissed me on the lips. "Thank you. You're a nice man." Then she hopped out and joined her son.

I was somewhat taken aback but not totally shocked. It's happened before. There's something about the combination of the mythic lifestyle, the proximity of the carefully made double-sleeper bed, and the privacy that makes the truck, under certain conditions, a jolly fine aphrodisiac. It's an immediate alternate universe.

We spent a pleasant afternoon on the beach. It was a lovely July day. Trevor loosened up, and we swam out to the float and splashed around playing Marco Polo. We got out and we skipped the flat stones that were all over the beach, and I bought him an ice cream sandwich. I sat for a while with Mrs. Howard and learned her first name was Alice. Later that afternoon they went back to town to camp in the empty house and I ate an excellent meatloaf and mashed potatoes at the local diner. I fell asleep reading *Mansfield Park* in my mushy motel bed.

A little after midnight I heard a knock on my door. I threw on a shirt and some shorts. "Who is it?"

"Alice Howard."

I opened the door. "Where's Trevor?"

"Asleep."

She lunged in, shut the door, and pulled me into her arms hugging me close for a long time. Then she turned her face up and kissed me. It was a deep, passionate, needful, longing kiss. Then she pulled my shirt off. She led me to the bed, took off my shorts, and lay next to me.

"Undress me, please."

I complied, with mixed feelings. Maybe she *was* crazy. On the other hand, she was obviously someone starved for a human touch and so was I. We made love quickly on the cheap motel bed. She came in like ninety seconds, which is something I'd never experienced before. We lay there awhile, silent, and then we started in again. About 3 a.m. we woke up and she said she had to leave. I kissed her goodnight and she was gone.

—

The next morning I called the TO, and he said the situation was developing and I was to continue standing by being paid waiting time and to expect developments soon. I was pretty sure Alice would be seriously regretting the night before, so I decided to fill my day elsewhere.

I hooked up my trailer and headed out of town to the Goodyear tire dealer. I'd been neglecting my tires, and that always spells trouble. I have eighteen tires and they're always in flux. The wear varies and the air pressure changes. Just checking that all tires have the required 95 psi is a dirty job that takes at least 45 minutes. I knew I needed a new inside left on my front trailer tandem and I wanted the tire guys to check my front tractor tires.

I've had lots of flats over the years. Usually when it happens I hear a bang like a close-up pistol shot and then, depending on which tire blew, a certain amount of new vibration. If I'm running empty and the flat is a trailer tire, I won't feel much at all. If it's a drive tire on my tractor and I'm full, then I'll feel it a lot. I can drive a certain distance with one of these flats but not far. The flat tends to heat up, and if it gets too hot it will catch fire. The last flat I had was in Texas. I heard the bang and saw the gator in my mirror taking up the roadway. I pulled over to check it out. It was the Fourth of July and I was in the middle of nowhere. I looked up and saw I was right at an exit. Next to the ramp was a Goodyear truck tire dealer. I limped over to the yard and there was a sign with a phone number for emergency service. I called it and ten minutes later a guy showed up from his holiday barbecue and changed my tire in about seven minutes. That's the way to get a flat. The bill was $600: $350 for the tire and $250 for the holiday service call. That's why I lease my truck. I don't buy tires and I don't pay for repairs.

The real problem with flats is when one of the front tires blows out. All of a sudden the truck lurches hard over to the side that blew. It grabs the steering wheel and yanks it. Hard. There's no holding it. The tractor goes into a rapid deceleration and the trailer momentum has a tendency to want to ride over the tractor. The range of possibilities is that the truck will go into the adjacent lane out of control, careen off the shoulder and into a gully, or jackknife and flip. Other trucks or four-wheelers anywhere near will be sucked into mayhem. All drivers are terrified of front-wheel blowouts. For four-wheelers driving next to trucks, I'd recommend never staying near the front wheels with your car. When passing a truck, pass it fast and get ahead of it. I've had one front-wheel blowout in my career. It happened in South Carolina, naturally, late at night. I was lucky and I wrestled it to a stop without incident. I had to call TC for a Comchek that night for over $1,000. When I was finally towed to the tire place, I purchased two brand-new Michelin X Line steering tires. Never again, I hoped. Trucker legend has it that flat tires come in threes.

———

I returned to Lakeland in the early evening and ate my dinner again at the diner. It was fish-and-chips night. Then I walked back to the motel.

I'd been thinking of our little romp pretty much all day. Alice was sweet and vulnerable, and I figured I'd pretend the whole thing never happened. Movers aren't supposed to sleep with their shippers. I lay down on my motel bed and tried to sleep when just after midnight I heard the knock on the door I'd been half hoping to hear and half dreading. Alice was there, wearing a short skirt and tank top. I pulled her inside, shut the door, and pushed her against it while reaching under her skirt. She grabbed my arms and pushed me onto the bed, yanking at my clothes.

Afterward, we lay in bed talking, making love, talking. I didn't really learn anything new. Her husband was a control freak with no emotional life, no sex drive, and on a career track. That was pretty much it. Alice was a warm woman whose self-confidence, never strong, had been shattered by him.

On day three the TO said to continue standing by, with pay. Alice and Trevor went back to the beach. I drove to the Brunswick pool table factory and took a tour. Making a pool table was pretty interesting, but I couldn't really pay attention. I was looking at all the skilled white union workers knowing they were dead men walking. All I was wondering was how long it would take for this factory to move offshore.

That night, Alice showed up again just after midnight. She was wearing a short print dress. When I opened the door she pushed me back and put her finger to her mouth, imploring me to be quiet. She walked back to the doorway, turned around to face me, and slowly released the shoulder straps of her dress. She turned again and let the dress drop to the floor. She was wearing nothing underneath. I stood there mesmerized as she told me to lie down.

"Do you want me?" she asked.

"I do," I croaked.

On day four the TO called me and said the load was going back to Nebraska. I returned to the Howard place to say good-bye.

Alice and Trevor were loading the car for the trip back. Alice sent Trevor into the house to get something and we talked for about a minute, maybe less.

"So," I said, "it's back to the base?"

"Yes. Incarceration is better than exile."

"Are those your choices? Don't you have any others?"

"As a matter of fact, I don't. That part of this conversation is over. I want to thank you though. I knew there was something fantastic and strong and feminine and powerful inside me. I don't think I'll ever experience it again, but I'll hold it close to me for the rest of my life. It's locked in here and it belongs to me and nobody else."

"That's it?"

"That's it. Thanks again. Have a safe trip."

I never saw her again.

Chapter 12
PARADISE

There are some places that regular people just shouldn't go if they haven't developed a taste for low company. This motel is one of them. I found the place by accident many years ago, having popped off an airport exit looking for a place to park. I was sitting at the light at the bottom of the ramp, and across the street I saw a line of bedbug trucks. Mayflower, Arpin, Wheaton, North American, Atlas, Allied, National, Bekins. It looked like a convention. I pulled in, parked, and went into the office. The sign there said to check in at the bar. Excellent info. Into the bar I went and sat down. The bartender looked at my van line shirt, nodded, and brought me a Coors from the tap.

"I'll be with you in a couple of minutes, driver. You OK with that?"

"I am now," I answered, looking at the beer. The décor was perfect—shirts pinned to the walls and ceiling, hundreds of them. Every shirt was from a moving company. I saw one for Pickfords (London and Nottingham), another for Leos/UmZug (Düsseldorf), and one for Froesch (Russia). Hot diggity dog, this was movers' heaven. It's the only place I know in the whole USA where movers rule the roost. Looking around I could tell by the tired eyes, the big arms, and the T-shirts that everyone in this bar was a mover. It was love at first sight. Ever since then I'll stop there if I'm even close to it, close being within two hundred miles.

On this particular trip I had settled my rig in the capacious motel yard and headed straight to the bar to get a room. I've never once seen anyone at the reception desk. I hadn't been here in a while, but the décor hadn't changed. I sat down and looked around for a Callahan Bros. or Joyce Van Lines shirt, but it would've taken me a week to find one. Well, I was going to fix that.

I sat on an empty bar stool near the cash register and waited to check in. It was early evening, and the place was crowded but manageable. Within a minute or two the bartender dropped a draft beer in front of me and went away. A minute or two later a guy sat down next to me and started talking. This is a total trucker thing I never experience anywhere else: Whether it's a bar, restaurant, truckstop, or repair shop, a trucker will just start talking to another trucker without introductions, names, or social niceties. It's almost like he's continuing a conversation that got interrupted. This driver was a white guy about my age. Maybe a little younger. All of them are younger.

"Joyce," he said, reading my shirt. "That's in Connecticut, right?"

"Yup."

"I heard the guy that owns that place is a maniac."

"Yup."

"What would he say if he knew you were here?"

"He'd probably say he wants to fly out here and put his company shirt on the wall. Problem is he weighs four hundred pounds and his shirt would take up a doorway."

"Been here before?"

"Nope," I lied. I wanted to hear what this guy had to say. "It looks like I'll be here again, though. What's the deal?"

"Just what you see, bedbugger heaven. Need anything? That guy on the end there will sell you walkboards, dollies, pads . . . The guy next to him will sell you drugs. The guy at the four top in the corner has labor and packing material. His buddy sitting across from him has firearms and hookers. This is the Mall of America for movers. Discount prices too, since everything's been jacked."

"What are you? The sales rep?"

"Not at all. Just giving you the lay of the land. I come here all the time. Your truck is safe. The stuff doesn't get jacked exactly. It's more like a guy's stuck down here and is in arrears back at the office and needs some cash. So he'll sell off his fifteen-hundred-dollar walkboards for two hundred to the guy over there. He'll sell them to you for four. He's the middleman."

"How's a guy going to load without his walkboards?"

"Mostly it's guys that are quitting. Before they drop the trailer and take off, they'll sell off all the equipment. In the good old days there were guys that would buy the load too. That's when people had TVs and stereo systems that were worth something. Nowadays a new flat screen at Best Buy will run you a couple hundred maybe, the sound systems are in their phones, and their furniture all comes from IKEA. The aftermarket's gone in household goods. Nothing people move these days is worth shit."

"I've noticed."

"Me too. The moves get more expensive, and the stuff they own is garbage. This is a great place, though. The only thing you can't do is drop your trailer. A dropped trailer is considered abandoned, and it will be gone quicker than you can say mañana. I hear the hardwood floors from a Kentucky 53 are a household fashion statement south of Nogales."

"You seem to know a lot."

"I do. I've been running Up and Down since '88."

"I've been running the coasts since 1980, mostly the Top, though. I don't run the Dime too much. We do corporate execs. All pack and loads. Mostly big ones."

"I'm all snowbird CODs. Lots of little ones. Scottsdale, Sun City. Terrible places. Camp Verde's still kind of funky."

"I did that snowbird work with North American for a while. Eight shipments with nine deliveries in three days type of thing. Very wearing. Lots of digging shipments out of the nose."

"There is that. On the other hand, I couldn't spend all that time with a shipper. On a big pack and load you can be with the shipper for like a week, right?"

"Sometimes."

"Ever nail a hot shipper on one of those fancy corporates?"

"Only once, but it wasn't a corporate, it was a military. Mr. Shipper was an army colonel. Mrs. Shipper was angry at him. I nailed her, not him. Actually, she nailed me.

"I'm happy for you. I've never even come close. Anyone who thinks driving's going to get you laid has read the wrong memo."

"What else do I need to know about this place?"

"A few things. Always wear your van line shirt. They've got twenty-four-hour armed security here. They're here to protect the movers and the trucks. The story I heard is that the owner used to be a road driver years ago and has a soft spot. Nobody will mess with you here if you've got your shirt on. The hookers and the dealers understand that. It's open season on everyone else, though. In other words, it's the opposite of the world outside. The other thing is to ask for the mover's rate. The posted room rate is eighty-nine dollars. You'll pay forty-nine and get a room with a fridge and a key to the pool. Everyone else has to pay extra for those. Last thing is, don't go outside the property. This is a nasty neighborhood, but it's safe inside. The food here is excellent, and there's nothing outside anyway except a Mickey D. You need to go somewhere? Ask the bartender for a taxi. They've got the right guys who will bring you back in one piece."

"Thanks for all the info."

We shook hands. "Wait till you check out the jukebox. No George Strait or Waylon Jennings. It's all Led Zeppelin and Grateful Dead. Welcome to the alternate universe."

The bartender turned up with another Coors. Before handing it over he asked, "I'm assuming you're parked and off duty, right?"

"Oh yeah. Those days are long gone."

"Not around here. Not yet, anyway. You checking in? It's forty-nine bucks with a room in front near your rig. I saw you talking to Kurt. He give you the lowdown?"

"He did."

"Welcome, driver. I'm Bill. You're with Joyce in Connecticut? Ever run into a driver named Perry Walker?"

"I know Perry. He just retired."

"Perry's a real gentleman. He'd sit here all night drinking club soda, soaking in the scene. Told me this was the only bar he'd been in in his whole life and didn't think he'd need to see another one."

"That's Perry. Church every Sunday, even on the road. He's home in Texas. He's got cancer. Never had a drop of liquor or a cigarette pass his lips in sixty-five years."

"Tell Perry I said hello if you see him. If you need anything, let me know. Enjoy yourself."

"Actually, I have a question. What's the protocol for getting a shirt up on the wall?"

"Just bring one in. The whole bar does a shot of Jack Daniel's together and we put it up. I know for sure Joyce isn't up there. It's about time."

"Thanks. I'll come back later for the ceremony."

I finished my beer and went to my room. It was squeaky clean, though it did smell a bit like cigarette smoke. But hell, I smoke. I took a long hot shower. The water pressure was superb. As I toweled off I grabbed my phone. I was dying to call Willie Joyce.

"Willie, guess where I am?"

"Hmm, let me see. The two lesbians who had a fight and split the shipment up when I was unloading? Naw, that was Northampton. Oh, I know . . . where the guy shipped his own golf cart for driving around. Had a custom paint job and a lot of extras. Reminded me of Rodney Dangerfield in *Caddyshack*. Nope. That was Sun City. Where are you?"

"Think harder. I know there's more in that brain than load plans and bogus driver debits."

"Wait. I remember a bar. Lot helpers. Hookers."

"Come on, Willie. That could be anywhere. Think harder."

I told him, and he said, "Hey, I know that place. That's the bar with the moving company shirts all over the ceiling. I loved that place. They had a guy out by the pool selling dollies."

"Bingo, driver. Bad news, though. There's no Joyce Van Lines shirt here on the wall. I consider that a serious deficiency. So does the bartender. He knows Perry Walker."

"He can't know Perry. Perry doesn't go to bars."

"He goes to this one."

"Good for Perry. Listen, Finn, we need our shirt on that wall. What does it take?"

"You have to fly out here and put it up. They've got shirts here with movers from Germany, Russia. Everywhere."

"I should have left my shirt there back in '79."

"It would have said North American. That's no good. How fast can you get out here? I'm unloading up north tomorrow and can swing back the day after. They have a ceremony. You'll have to buy shots of Jack Daniel's for the bar and then they'll put it up. You should see the parking lot. It looks like the AMSA annual meeting. The guy at the pool has expanded. He's now selling walkboards and Oxycontin. You should see the girls."

"You know I'd love to. Damn. Glad to hear the good old place is still going strong. You've made my day. I can't do it, but I'm glad you're there."

"For sure? What's the point of owning a company if you can't break out for a laugh? You're a multimillionaire, for crissakes, and you never have any fun. You can help me drop this mini day after next, and we'll spend the night here, have a couple pops at the bar, put up the shirt, and you're back in Oxford in the afternoon."

"Can't do it."

"Won't do it, laddie. I know the difference. You should too."

"I do. I just get so tired."

"OK. I'll go as your proxy. I'll bill you two hundred and fifty dollars for the Jack Daniel's toast."

"That's cheaper than me flying out there."

"Don't be such a spoilsport, Willie. I'll bet there's never been a van line owner in that bar. Much less a van line owner who used to be a driver. You'd be king for a night. A real-life hero with a hundred long-haul drivers in the room. Face it, Willie, you go to the AMSA conferences and they treat you like a leper because you came up through the hawsehole. Here they'd carry you around on their shoulders. We'd need a lot of guys to do that, frankly, but we're movers. We could do it."

"Sure. And like the king I'd be stuck with the whole bar bill instead of just the Jack Daniel's."

"That's what kings do, Will. They feed the peasants on feast days."

"It's tempting, but no. It's crazy busy here. I can't get away."

"I'm done with the sales pitch. I'm going over to have a beer and check out dolly prices. Goodnight, Willie."

"Be safe, laddie. Hey . . . I'm glad you called. I'm glad you asked."

"I know you are, Will. One of these days you're going to need to say yes before it's all over. For both of us. You know that, right?"

"We'll see. Maybe one of these days . . ."

Chapter 13
THE GREAT
WHITE MOVER

I was loading yet again, a GE exec. This time it was a Boston to Santa Barbara pack and load and looked like another easy $20,000 layup. I'm now one of those ghost movers I wondered about years ago. The guys with the nondescript white Peterbilts and the squeaky clean, brand-new unmarked trailers who strut up to the fuel desk like they're doing Flying J a favor.

I was finishing up in Boston when I got the call from Willie. He told me to get down to Connecticut, drop the Santa Barbara trailer, pick up another one, and be in Storrs for a widow to pack and load 22,000 pounds the next morning. I laughed and told him to find someone else.

"Willie, I've been loading all day, it's five o'clock. If I was going to do this crazy shipment I'd have to drive three hours to Waterbury, drop the trailer, put equipment onto the new trailer, plus packing material, which is a two- or three-hour job, arrange for six or seven helpers, get the paperwork, get a tare weight, and then drive two more hours up to Storrs. I'll get to bed around three a.m., no food, no shower, to spend the next day packing and loading twenty-two thousand, which even with seven guys will take twelve hours minimum. No way."

Willie laughed back. "It gets worse, Finn. You're unloading Sunday in New Mexico."

"Which Sunday?"

"This Sunday."

"You're crazy, Willie. Today is Tuesday. It's twenty-two hundred miles. That means seven hundred and thirty miles on Thursday, seven hundred and thirty miles Friday, and seven hundred and thirty miles on Saturday. I've got a truck, Willie, I drive it myself. You think Scotty just beams me out into the desert?"

"You're not calculating this correctly, Finn. You drive three hundred miles Wednesday night and three hundred miles early Sunday morning. That means you only have to do five hundred and thirty each day. Think of the revenue. I'll put Santa Barbara on a haulaway, and you can pick it up when you're done with Mrs. McMahon. You'll make twenty grand on this and another twenty on the Santa Barbara. That's forty grand in fourteen days. That's almost as much as I make."

"But I'll be dead, Willie."

"You won't be dead, you'll be rich. This is perfectly doable. You won't even have to fudge your logs." Willie loves this crazy stuff because he gets to play superman. "Who else would be able to handle a full load, at peak rates, on twelve hours' notice, in the middle of July, for a grieving widow? Nobody but us. Joyce Van Lines, the Professionals. Wait until you meet Mrs. McMahon, she's a hoot."

"I don't want to meet her, Willie. I want to get some sleep."

"I've got nobody else, Finn. I told her all about you. The Great White Mover, my number one driver, my old buddy from back in the day."

"I thought Tom Sturtevant was your number one driver?"

"Sturtevant was number one yesterday. Ancient history. He's in Chicago anyway, I checked. Listen, her husband died *this morning* . . . Besides, I told her *we'd be there*."

I can hear the ice in his voice. I know Willie very well. If he had to pull the trailer by hand all by himself, a Joyce truck would be there at 8 a.m., and whoever didn't help him will have become a non-person. Willie's life is full of ex-friends who've crossed him in some minor way just like this. For some reason I can't explain, I don't want to join the ranks of Willie's ex-friends. Fortunately, for some reason Willie can't explain, I often get a pass that others don't get. Regardless of that mutual understanding we each stay in character. It's my turn now, in this decades-old pantomime, to push back.

"You know why everyone in this business hates you, Willie? It's because of stuff like this. You give this lady your word of honor you'll be there, and then you expect someone else to execute it. It's not right. Jesus Christ carried his own cross up the hill. He didn't ask one of the apostles to do it."

"That's a very interesting analogy, Finn. Your theme is martyrdom, like what you're doing right now. I'm offering you the best turn I've seen in years, and you want to take a shower and eat and sleep? That's pathetic. I'm talking forty grand here."

"Willie, I know you. When it's all totted up, it won't be forty grand. And another thing—I know you never hear this when people say it to you, and I know a zillion people *have* said it to you, but here it is again: There's more to life than high-paying loads."

"That's true, Finn. Right now I've got a widow who's relying on my company to move her tomorrow. It's not about the money anymore. If it makes you feel any better, you're right about everything; everyone does hate me, and when I give my word I do expect the people around me to execute. That's why they're called *employees*. I don't care what they have to go through. Want to know something else? I sleep like a baby every night."

"That's because nobody who works for you gets any sleep at all. And I'm not your employee. I'm your contractor, and this kind of stunt is why I'm a contractor. I'm never going to put you in a position to fire me, because if I did, you would eventually fire me for some reason. You'd be out one more friend, and Willie, you don't have that many friends. You can starve me for loads if you want, you can take your truck back, but you can't fire me."

"What I'm trying to do is *load* you, not starve you. You said you wanted to make some money. This is real money."

"This isn't about me making money. This is about *you* making promises to people. This is about *you* being the man who says yes to the impossible. I admire it, in a way, though I admire it more when I'm not the fall guy. OK, tell you what: You pay for the haulaway and pay me the full line haul from Boston on the Santa Barbara, and I'll fulfill your promise to Mrs. McGann."

"Dream on, Finn. I will pay the haulaway from Boston to New Mexico. That's twenty-five hundred out of my pocket. You'll get paid from Farmington, New Mexico, to Santa Barbara on the other one. The shipper's name is McMahon, not McGann, so please don't be disrespectful. The lady's a widow, for crissakes. Anyway, on McMahon you'll get the line haul and the packing. I'll give you the whole thing."

"That's nice of you, Will. On McMahon I'm *doing* the whole thing."

"Are we done here? Don't worry about what time you get down here tonight. Pete and Rob will be there till midnight at least, and they'll have your paperwork. And to lighten your load, I'll have them pull the packing material. It'll all be ready on the dock. You're not the only guy in this organization losing a little sleep. I sure wish I was going with you. One of these days I'm going to pack it all in and just get me a big ol' Peterbilt and do nothing but haul high-tariff pack and loads . . ."

I've heard Willie rhapsodize about giving up his multimillion-dollar business and going back on the road with his big ol' Peter-bilt too many times. It will never happen. He's going to die of a stroke, on the phone, happy as a puppy, cajoling some poor sap into bringing the same commitment to his van line that he has. When the unfortunate day comes and his veins just give up, bang! It'll all be over. Some of us will be sad, some of us will be relieved, and some of us will feel unmoored. The thing about Willie, and people like him, is that he gives purpose to the lives of people who haven't, for whatever reason, found their own purpose. Willie's a Pied Piper for unmoored individuals because he has all the answers, pays all the bills, and offers a modicum of security. In return he demands complete loyalty.

Naturally, I was in Storrs the next morning at 8 a.m.

The McMahon shipment wasn't a corporate job. She was a cash-paying customer, what we call a COD. The McMahons had lived in New Mexico for thirty years. Mr. McMahon was a profes-sor of some kind and a consultant to the Native American com-munity near the Four Corners. When he was diagnosed with cancer, he told his wife he wanted to move back to Connecticut for treatment. Mrs. McMahon, in ill health herself, was not in favor, but she dutifully called the movers and arranged for the move back to Storrs. The McMahons loaded their 22,000 pounds of house-hold goods, including several thousand Native American artifacts, and went east. They weren't looking for the Next Big Thing; they were looking for good health care and a closer family circle. They settled into an old white colonial house with black shutters. A few months after their arrival, Professor McMahon went to the hospital complaining of a sore throat. They diagnosed a mild infection, and since he was in chemo, they admitted him for the night. This was on a Sunday. On the Monday he contracted a staph infection, probably from the hospital, but who knows. Tuesday morning he was dead.

Tuesday afternoon Mrs. McMahon called Joyce Van Lines. She was going back to New Mexico at once, she said, and needed to arrange everything that day. Willie himself came out to do the estimate, since everyone else was busy. She told him he needed to get a truck and crew there the next morning for a full pack and load, and the driver needed to be in New Mexico on Sunday. Willie agreed to all of it.

When we arrived, I knocked on the door, heard a faint "Come in," and walked in with my crew. There she was, on the sofa, half supine, wheezing. The eight of us looked at her. She looked at us for a moment and sat up. Regardless of everything else, Willie was right about Mrs. McMahon being a character. She was a heavy woman in her early seventies with dyed jet-black hair. Perhaps heavy is not quite accurate; gargantuan might be better. Mrs. McMahon had piercing, smart, gray eyes, a permanent sardonic grin, and a plastic hose attached to her nostrils. There was a big tank of oxygen in the corner of the room and about a hundred feet of hose coiled up leading to her nose. When I say a big oxygen tank, I mean the industrial ones about five feet tall. Mrs. McMahon eyed me with a knowing half grin.

"Mr. Murphy, I presume. Your employer, Mr. Joyce, tells me you're the Great White Mover. What exactly does that mean? Who are the rest of these people? I like to be on a first-name basis with anyone going through my underwear drawers, my basement, and my bathroom. Step up, gentlemen!"

"Well, Mrs. McMahon," I started out, "this is Nate, Carl, Mike, Carlos, Bobby, Lou, and Waldo."

"Ha! I don't believe any of it. Did you ever get on the phone with one of those call centers in India? Some guy you can barely understand says, 'Good afternoon, thank you for your call, my name is Ralph,' when you know his name is really Runjeev or Gohar or something. No aliases! What about you, Mr. Good-looking Black Man?"

"I really am Nate. I was christened Nathaniel."

"What about you?"

"I'm Carlos, ma'am. Mike is Mike, That's Francisco, Roberto, Luis, and nobody knows Waldo's real name. We've tried for years, ma'am. He won't tell anybody."

"You, Waldo, come over here."

"Si, yes, oui?" Waldo stammered in heavily accented something or other.

"Look at me, Mr. Waldo. I can't breathe, I can barely see, and I know I'm on short time here on planet Earth. I lost my husband of fifty-five years yesterday. I don't broach any bullshit. What's your real name?"

"Frederico."

"Excellent. You can all call me Mrs. McMahon. Now you, Mr. Great White Mover, there's a question on the table. Are you Kiowa, Southern Cheyenne, one of those crazy Utes? With a name like that you sound like a chief."

"I'm a hundred percent Irish, Mrs. McMahon. I'm also the chief of this team today. The term Great White Mover is a kind of joke. I *am* like an Indian chief, in that I'm doomed to extinction. There are so few white drivers left in this business, Mr. Joyce started calling me the Great White Mover. He thinks I'm going to be the last one. It's evocative of a bygone time. It's not a racist thing."

"I didn't think it was a racist thing. I imagine you're pretty ecumenical down in the laboring trenches."

"Essentially nonsectarian, ma'am."

"Excellent again. A man with a vocabulary. Evocative. Nonsectarian. We'll get along, I think, Mr. Great White Mover. Should I call you Mr. Great or Mr. White or Mr. Mover?"

"Finn will do fine."

"Finn? Like a resident of Suomi or the directional appendage of a piscine?"

"Suomi, ma'am."

"Good, Mr. Finn. Now, don't you gentlemen have work to do? I'm out of here today, remember? No excuses. Everything is going in the truck except for the suitcase next to me, the oxygen tanks, and the contents of my medicine cabinet. You mess with any of those and it'll be a short day, because I'll be dead. I have lunch ordered for 1 p.m. I've ordered a bunch of crap from the deli slathered with cheese and unidentifiable meat along with an array of liquid carbonated sugar poisons. That will suffice?"

Nate broke in laughing, "That's perfect, ma'am. Thank you."

"You're welcome, Mr. Nate. If you guys work assiduously, I'll arrange for some dinner also. I suspect we'll all be together until the evening. If you don't work assiduously, you can go hungry. Unfortunately, or maybe not, I learned about food too late in life to do anything about it. I'm living with the consequences, barely. It's an interesting existential question: If I had learned about food thirty years ago, would I have changed my habits? Probably not. People don't change their habits, do they, Mr. Nate?"

"Not often, ma'am."

"Do you see that long hose over there, gentlemen? I can get to any corner of the house to check on you, and checking I will do. No goldbricking or I'll catch you. I'm smart and I'm nosy. We will be finished today. That's not negotiable."

The crew scattered to start their work. We'd all worked together before on full-service moves, and they knew exactly what to do. I sat down with Mrs. McMahon and was going over some details when a bald, slim man of about forty came in.

"Ah, Kevin. Glad you're here. This is Finn. He's the driver. Calls himself the Great White Mover. Finn, Kevin is my son. He lives over in Danbury." We shook hands.

"I'm pleased to meet you, Kevin. I'm very sorry for your loss."

"Thank you. I'll be here to help Mom through the move. I'll also be in New Mexico."

"That's great. Your mother and I were just going over some stuff. Here's the way I understand things so far: First, we need to finish everything today. I've got a large, very experienced crew, but there are a lot of items here. We'll probably be here until nine or ten tonight."

"We expected that," said Kevin.

"OK. Second, I understand I need to be in New Mexico on Sunday morning at eight."

"That's correct." Kevin again.

"OK. Now you know what that entails, right? Today is Wednesday. I have no wiggle room. If I get a flat tire, blow a gasket, hit some traffic, that deadline might be threatened. I'm not making excuses. I intend to be there, but it's a very close call."

"We know," said Kevin. "We're going too."

"Excuse me?"

"We're going too. The reason I'm late this morning is I had to go pick up the motor home. The oxygen company is coming over later. We're going to fill the Winnebago with tanks and head to New Mexico as soon as you guys are finished tonight. Mom can't fly. We'll meet you there Sunday morning."

"Really? You two are quite a pair. Can I ask why it has to be Sunday?"

Kevin looked over at his silent mother. "You can ask. We've all asked. She won't say. When Dad died yesterday, all she said was 'Let's go. We can be there by Sunday.' She's a force of nature. I don't recommend trying to thwart her."

"I've no intention of trying to thwart her. My job is to do whatever your mom wants me to do. The job was explained to me last night by Mr. Joyce. I'm on your team on this. We're partners."

"That's very nice to hear."

"You know it's probably illegal to transport that much oxygen in a Winnebago?"

"We already researched it, Mr. Finn," chimed in Mrs. McMahon. "It's so illegal we're not telling the oxygen company. They're going to put the tanks in the garage. I was going to ask you to get your guys to load them into the camper. Will you do that?"

"We'll do that. I've got straps and tie-downs. We'll figure out a way to keep them from shifting. I'm going to start the packing in the dining room, Mrs. McMahon. I like to pack the high-value items myself. Mr. Joyce said something about Indian artifacts. Can we go in there and look things over?"

"You go in with Kevin. He can explain. I'll be right along. It takes me a while to get anywhere."

Kevin and I walked across the house to the dining room. He looked at me and smiled a sad smile. "She's not crazy, you know."

"No, she's not. I think she's wonderful."

"Really?"

"Yes."

"You've no idea how much better I feel hearing that from you. She *is* wonderful. Her body is falling apart, but her mind and her will are spot on. I really don't know why everything needs to be done in such a hurry. I think it has to do with this stuff." Kevin indicated the dining room. Every wall was filled with pottery shards. Some were in the shapes of animals, some were jars, some plates, some looked like toys. There were thousands of them. "My father was an archaeologist. He went to New Mexico for his post-doc and hooked up with a native group around the Four Corners. You never met my dad, but he was as remarkable as my mom. The Indians trusted him. He went back to UConn for a couple years, but he found his home and his calling in New Mexico. I grew up there, and Dad worked with the Indians. He set up a system for their artifacts. He got rid of the thieves and the rogue traders. Some of their good stuff goes for hundreds of thousands of dollars. Back in the seventies people were just stealing everything."

"What's all this stuff here?"

"Junk. There's not an unbroken item in this collection. There are places in the desert where it's piled in heaps. Dad didn't care if they were broken. He knew what the designs meant and what the purpose was, and that was what was important to him. He was never what you would call a collector of artifacts. He hated collectors. When he got sick he felt he had to move back to Connecticut. My aunts are here, the hospital is here. Of course Mom didn't want to go, but she did. They've only been here two months. We've got boxes from the first move in the basement still untouched. Dad was in chemo, and Mom can barely breathe in this humidity. They never settled in. Mom, as you know, has no intention of settling in."

"What about you, Kevin? Can you just drop everything and do this?"

"Well, I am dropping everything. I've got three young kids at home, and it's summer vacation. My wife's been great, but this—this move today, delivering Sunday, driving Mom across the country in a camper loaded with illegal oxygen—has flipped her out. She thinks my mom is being overbearing and selfish."

Mrs. McMahon lurched into the room, heaving and wheezing on her walker. "What's my son been telling you about me? That I'm an overbearing, selfish old woman?"

I smirked at her. "It's not always about you, Mrs. McMahon. Kevin was telling me about the artifacts. My scientific interest is limited, to be honest. I'm a mover. I care about transporting stuff safely. When I pack dishes and art objects, I'm supposed to write an inventory of existing damage. So if there's a chip in a Waterford glass before I pack it, I make a note so I don't have to pay a damage claim at the other end. How do I write up this stuff? You could claim I broke it all and sue the van line for fifty million dollars."

Mrs. McMahon gave me a steely stare. "I don't want fifty million dollars, Mr. Great White Finn. Fifty million dollars sounds like a whole lot of trouble. What I really want is to be able to breathe. In fact, if I could breathe I'd give you fifty million dollars."

"Do you have fifty million dollars?"

"No. Unfortunately, I have fifty million pieces of clay from Indian garbage mounds. Want one?"

"No thanks."

"You're not into objects either. I can tell. Neither am I. This was my husband's stuff."

"Moving other people's things for twenty years has pretty

much cured me of acquisitiveness, Mrs. McMahon. I don't own much, and I don't even know where that is half the time."

"What *do* you want?"

"I want to get this house empty today and be in New Mexico by Sunday."

"That's all?"

"Right now, that's all."

"What about later?"

"Later? In my view, Mrs. McMahon, American culture underrates the value of short-term goals. We can talk about other goals in New Mexico. After we're unloaded you can serve me cold Coronas and we'll talk about life, the universe, and everything. Right now we're running your train, and you said the house must be empty today. I think you're losing focus."

"Touché, Mr. Mover. They've all been waiting for me to lose focus, but my body's going to give way before my brain."

"Jeez. You and Willie Joyce must have got on like blood brothers. You're cut from the same cloth."

"Mr. Joyce and I share certain surface characteristics. We're overweight and intelligent. My interests are broader, however. I'd like to put my brain in that gorgeous black man's body over there. Then you'd see some focus."

"Oh, Nate's pretty focused himself. I don't think he'd do the trade. He's got a wife and two girlfriends. He carries around three cell phones. I'm going to write 'All contents broken' on each of these dishpacks with the artifacts. Are you OK with that? You're going to have to sign it that way."

"Fine. The meaning of them all died with my husband. Not even the Indians know what they mean. It's all from trash piles made three thousand years ago. They were a different people back then. It's like when Charlton Heston found that doll in *Planet of the Apes*. Make sure you put the artifact boxes at the very end of the load. They have to come off first, OK?"

"OK."

"It's very important they come off first. Don't mess it up."

"Yes, Mrs. McMahon. I'll make sure. I won't mess it up."

I went to work. Kevin went to work. My crew was at work. Mrs. McMahon staggered back to her sofa and grabbed a full-face oxygen mask connected to a smaller tank.

Mrs. McMahon slept on and off most of the day and evening on her sofa. She didn't roam the house with her extra-long hose to check on my crew, but she did have a sardonic comment whenever any of the men passed through the living room. I think it took everything she had just to breathe. We finished loading at nine thirty that night. The house was empty and the truck was full. So full we had to strap the patio table to the back door of the trailer. The crew filed inside to say good-bye. Nate, who'd been yammering with Mrs. McMahon most of the day, tapped her gently on the shoulder. Mrs. McMahon woke up.

"Ma'am, we're done. Did it all today, just like you wanted. Good luck to you."

"Nice job, gentlemen. I thank you." She reached into her bag and pulled out an envelope. "This is three hundred and fifty dollars. That's fifty for each man. Split it up in front of me, Nate, and hand it out. Mr. Finn will get his tip if he beats me to New Mexico. You sure you don't want to trade your body for my brain there, Nate?"

"If there was a way to share both, ma'am, I'd do it. I could use some brains, and your body sure as shit is wearin' out."

"Nate!" I cut in.

"You leave Nate alone, Mr. Finn. We're family."

"OK, Mrs. M. You're the boss."

"I'm always the boss. You gentlemen take care of yourselves. You Spaniards or whatever you are—learn some English! You're going to be an embarrassment to your kids. You don't want that."

"You sure don't," Kevin said. He was exhausted too, but smiling.

I did the three hundred miles that night. I-80 through Pennsylvania is a horrible 311 miles of construction zones. It's just like I-40 east out of California. The roadwork never ends; it's orange cones and steep hills the whole way and a nightmare at night. In a way it's worse than the Rocky Mountains: sure, the Rockies have hills, but the Rockies aren't that wide. They're maybe seventy miles, so they eventually end. In Pennsylvania the hills never quit. One late night a few years ago, on I-80 outside of Clarion, I saw a big truck off to the side of the road, catty-corned. It didn't look right. I pulled over, stopped, and walked up to the truck. The windshield was smashed and I saw the leg of a deer hanging over the hood. Where the driver was supposed to be I saw the deer's head. Everything was perfectly still and quiet. I didn't look any further. I saw police lights coming around the bend so I knew someone had already called it in, so I left. I knew what had happened. I hoped it was quick for both of them.

I crawled into my sleeper around 5 a.m. somewhere near Lock Haven, Pennsylvania. This wasn't a logbook nightmare, yet, because I logged my loading time as off duty. I got to Vandalia, Illinois, by midnight Thursday. I've done the cross-country thing so many times now the bloom is pretty much off the rose, though I do still get a twinge crossing the Big Ditch at St. Louis, which I did Friday morning. The first time I did that was with Willie back in 1979. Jeez. I pulled into the truckstop at Limon, Colorado, on Saturday around 6 p.m. and was putting another thousand dollars' worth of fuel into the tanks when my phone rang.

"Driver Murphy here. On schedule."

"Finn, it's Kevin McMahon."

"Hello, Kevin. Where are you guys?"

"She didn't make it, Finn. I'm at a funeral home in Salina, Kansas. Mom went aft to take a nap. When I pulled into Salina she was gone."

"Christ, Kevin. I'm so sorry."

"Yeah. Me too. We talked about it on the way out here. I'm supposed to meet you at the house tomorrow morning. You're still on schedule?"

"I am."

"I'll see you tomorrow morning at eight, then."

"Kevin, if you leave now, you'll barely make it."

"I'll make it. I've got to stop at a friend's house in Farmington first. He picked up my dad's ashes from the FedEx office. My mom had them shipped there from Watertown."

"What are you going to do about your mom?"

"She'll stay in Salina. In the refrigerator."

"You're sure about all this, right?"

"I'm sure."

"OK, Kevin. You're the boss now. I'll be there, but I have to stop too, to pick up labor."

"You won't need any labor."

"What? You and I are going to unload? I'll need to pick up some help."

"You won't need any help. Trust me on this. Just get rolling."

"Kevin . . . first your dad, now your mom. It's only been a couple days. Are you all right?"

"Yeah. No. Maybe. This is what I have to do. Please don't talk to me. Just be there, and don't bring anyone."

"I'll be there, Kevin. I'll be there. I won't bring anyone."

I had a bitch of a drive ahead of me. It was only 400 miles to Farmington, but I was off the interstate in Limon, and it was flat back roads for 150 miles to Walsenburg and then 250 miles of serious twists and turns and ups and downs, in the dark, to Farmington. There's a reason these Indian reservations are out in the middle of nowhere. The reason is, they're out in the middle of nowhere. I was pretty whacked-out tired, but nothing would make me be late for this delivery now. Mrs. McMahon was egging me on from the ether. My plan had been to sleep for five hours and do the last run through the night to get there about 7:30 a.m. Not anymore. I filled up with fuel, grabbed three large Dr Colas. and bought Doris Kearns Goodwin's *Team of Rivals* at the truckstop audiobook counter for forty bucks. I'd make it so long as the truck held up. I wasn't worried. A sort of confidence kicked in from somewhere. Whatever was going to happen would happen. I had the sweet feeling of knowing I was on the side of the angels.

I got into Farmington around 4 a.m. The McMahon house was another hour or so west. I found the place up in the hills. There were no other houses around. I parked my truck in the middle of the unpaved county road, set my flashers, and slept.

Around 9 a.m. somebody banged on my door. Once again, I didn't know where I was. I peeked through the curtain and saw I was surrounded by maybe a dozen pickup trucks. I threw on some clothes and emerged bleary-eyed into the New Mexico morning. A bunch of guys were standing around what appeared to be the lead truck. It was the only new one. My confidence from the day before carried me through. I walked up to the group.

"What's up?"

"Where's Mrs. McMahon and Kevin?" someone asked.

"Kevin's on his way."

"We'll wait." They all turned away. That was it.

A few minutes later a plume of dust appeared on the horizon. It slowly resolved into Kevin's Winnebago. He pulled up and greeted the man with the new pickup. I saw now they were all Indians.

"Are you ready?" asked the headman. "It's time to go. You have the artifacts?"

"They're in the back of the truck," said Kevin.

The headman turned to me. "Open it."

"Kevin?"

"Go ahead, Finn. This is why we're here. Open it up."

I unstrapped the patio table and opened the trailer. The entire last tier, except for some chowder, consisted of dishpack cartons containing the artifacts. There were fifteen of them. The men lined up and put them into the pickups in about two minutes.

"Let's go," said the headman.

"OK," said Kevin. "Finn, will you come with us? I've no family here, and I'd like you to come."

"Where are we going?"

"I've no idea. Please come."

"What about the shipment?"

"I don't know. This is why we're here. No more questions. Don't speak unless you're spoken to . . . and you won't be spoken to."

"OK, Kevin. I'm in."

Someone directed me to a pickup. Kevin went to the Winnebago and grabbed an urn from inside and got into another pickup. We headed west convoy fashion, with the headman in the lead. I sat in the middle of the bench seat between two Indians. The truck was old and battered, and the springs of the seat were poking through and kept digging into me. There was no air-conditioning, and we drove with the windows open. The dust from the convoy made it hard to breathe or see. Neither Indian spoke, either to each other or me. It wasn't long before I began to nod off.

We had driven for almost three hours when all the trucks pulled over for a piss call. When I got back to the pickup, the Indian in the passenger seat was gone. I got in, and the driver Indian handed me a bandanna. "Cover your eyes," he commanded. Then a bit more gently he said, "I'll answer a few questions on the ride, but you have to wear the bandanna."

"OK." I put on the blindfold and we started moving again.

"What are your questions?" asked the Indian.

"Why am I blindfolded?"

"We're going to a holy place. Nobody outside of our community can know where it is. Nobody from outside our community should even be going there." My driver, maybe I can almost call him my host, spoke perfect English with a high-pitched, singsong precision, like the Upper Midwest accent.

"Well, that rules out my next question, which was where are we going. What are we all doing?"

"We are carrying out a warrior burial ceremony for Professor McMahon."

"What's the big rush?"

"A warrior of our people is to be buried on the sixth day after his death. The ceremony is supposed to start in the morning. That's why it had to be today and why some were anxious about your arrival. I personally wasn't worried. You were the wild card because nobody knew you. Once I saw your truck I knew it would all fit together. These things arrange themselves. That's why you've been invited to the ceremony."

"I was? Nobody invited me. I thought Kevin asked me to come because he was scared."

"If you weren't invited you wouldn't be here. Kevin isn't scared. He knows exactly what's going on. Incidentally, if it makes you feel any better, he's blindfolded too."

"What about the artifacts?"

"When we bury our dead we provide them with items they'll need in the next world. As their life on Earth has been broken, so too are the gifts for the next world. That's why all of the objects are broken. Over the centuries many thousands of our gravesites have been pillaged by you moon crickets. This reflects badly upon our stewardship toward our ancestors' memories. McMahon recovered many gifts that were lost. Now they're going home. It's been a long time."

"What's a moon cricket?"

"You are a moon cricket. You have a pale face like the moon and a squeaky voice like a cricket. Also like a cricket, you don't know when or how to be quiet. I'm not speaking strictly personally here, you understand. Basically, it's anyone who is not one of us."

"Why did McMahon bring all that stuff to Connecticut?"

"No more questions." After about fifteen minutes we came to a stop and I heard doors slamming. The driver reached over and took off my blindfold. We were atop a mesa. The headman had changed from jeans and flannel shirt into some sort of ceremonial dress.

The warrior burial ceremony lasted until early evening. My hosts were explicit that I not divulge any details. I'm not going to.

———

The convoy dropped us off at the McMahon ranch a little after eight that night. The sun was starting its descent, and that beautiful soft desert red enveloped us. Kevin went into the house and brought out six Coronas, and we sat on the patio. He opened two of them and handed one to me.

"Cheers," he said.

"Cheers," I answered. "You know, it was supposed to be me and your mom sitting here drinking Coronas talking about life, the universe, and everything. That's not happening, but I think she'd be

OK with how it all turned out. I tell you, Kevin, this has been the weirdest move I've ever done." We clinked bottles. "What's next?"

"It's all going back. Tomorrow. You can start the truck and drop everything in storage at Joyce in Connecticut. It will take me years to sort it all out."

"You know this will cost you a fortune."

"I'm not worried about money. I'm an orphan now. Whatever connection I have left to my parents is in that truck, and it's going back with me. This house is finished for me. The Indian thing was their thing, not mine. I'll sell the ranch and keep what's in the moving van. Tomorrow I'll drop off the Winnebago and fly home. I have my marriage to repair, my kids to raise, my own life to live."

We finished our beers, and Kevin went back into the house and came out with a sleeping bag. "I'm going to sleep under the stars. I can't sleep in the house, and I won't sleep in Mom's bed in the camper. I've run out of options. You can sleep in the guest room if you want. I'll see you in the morning."

"Thanks," I said. "I'll sleep in my truck. I always sleep like a baby in there."

"Goodnight, Mr. Great White Mover. The Indians were really impressed with you. The name helped, of course. They all agreed that you actually were. That was some slick timing. They pretend they don't care about time, but when it comes to burials, they care only about time."

"Thanks for telling me. Right now, I'm thinking I am the Great White Mover after all. Good night, Kevin."

I took the four remaining beers back to my cab, cracked another, and called Willie at home.

"Hey, laddie," Willie said. "How's the desert?"

"Dry and hot, Willie. Tell me something: What's a salesman's commission these days for booking an interstate job?"

"Ten percent. Why do you ask?"

"'Cause I just booked twenty-two thousand pounds from Farmington, New Mexico, to Waterbury, Connecticut, for you."

"Really? Who? When?"

"Shipper McMahon. It leaves tomorrow. I'm hauling it too. Send the Santa Barbara all the way on the haulaway truck. You can have Phil unload it from Redlands."

"No way, Finn. Santa Barbara is your shipper. I'll put McMahon on a haulaway and bring it back here."

"No, Will, I'm bringing it back. It's non-negotiable."

"Nobody talks to me about non-negotiable. What'd you do, get religion out there?"

"Yeah, Will, I got religion."

"I'm not sure I like this. I could get pissed off. Don't you work for me?"

"Willie, I don't work for anyone. Not for a long time now. I'm bringing your truck back with McMahon's stuff. You can decide whether to like it or not."

"What if I decide I don't like it?"

"Then I'll fly home to Colorado. The Indians will hide the truck, and I can guarantee you won't find it for a thousand years."

"Indians? What Indians? What are you talking about?"

"Do I get the commission or not?"

"Commission? That's another issue. You're supposed to deliver Santa Barbara. Besides, you didn't earn a commission. This fell into your lap. What happened out there?"

"She died, Willie."

"Who died?"

"Mrs. McMahon."

"Oh."

"Oh is right. Do I get the commission?"

"She died on you? You kill a shipper and you're talking about a commission? That's cold-blooded."

"I was trained by you, Willie. Sometimes in the wild, babies eat their parents. Yes or no?"

". . . Yes, I suppose."

"Good boy, Willie. I'll see you on Friday. I'm going to take my time."

"Goodnight, laddie. Drive safe. I want you to know, I don't like this."

"Rubber side down all the way. Good night, Willie."

I hung up, cracked another beer and lit a smoke I'd bummed from one of the Indians. I watched the red sky turn to black. It happens real fast out here in the desert. So fast you wouldn't believe it if you weren't there.

I switched on the ignition, started the truck, and turned the air conditioner to high. Once the cab cooled down, the New Mexico night air would keep me comfortable until morning. I undressed, pulled back the filthy sheets, and crawled into the sleeper thinking over the past week. I was dog tired, had a satisfied customer, and just beat Willie Joyce out of twenty-five hundred bucks. That's a pretty good week in my world.

I lay quietly, snug in my cocoon, wondering why people think it's odd that a guy like me is a long-haul mover. I just helped another family navigate a major transition. What else could possibly matter? This is why we're all here: to help each other navigate.

My last thoughts before drifting off were about navigation. A mover's job is to shift people from where they are to where they're supposed to be. Lucky for me, every once in a while I find the place where I'm supposed to be too. It's a priceless gift that I only get when I'm out on the road.

It's the best job in the whole world.

EPILOGUE

Truckers aren't generally travelers on their off-time. The mundane domestic things that often annoy regular people are cherished by people like me. I love cleaning my little house, even the bathroom. Straightening out my garage or sorting odd socks will have me whistling with pleasure. We also do this with our trucks. It's a rare long-haul mover who doesn't keep his cab and trailer pristine and completely organized. I suppose it's a psychological reaction to the mess most of us have in our lives outside the truck.

One day not long ago, Willie had me run empty to Denver after a particularly lucrative quick turn to British Columbia. I got that one because I was the only driver in the fleet with a valid passport. I was annoyed to be deadheading fifteen hundred miles. Vancouver to Denver is the same mileage as Boston to Miami, but Boston to Miami is flat all the way. From Vancouver I get to experience the full catastrophe of American mountain driving. First is Snoqualmie Pass out of Seattle, and then there's the great granddaddy of all hills, called Cabbage, heading east out of Pendleton, Oregon. After that there are various bumps all the way to Fort

Collins, Colorado, any of which would have an East Coast driver reaching for his Valium.

After I arrived at the Joyce terminal in Erie, outside Denver, I knew why they'd sent me. Terminal is not quite the word for the Joyce facility there. It's actually a two-acre parking lot. There's no office or staff. It's there to spot or drop trailers and to arrange origin or destination services for drivers coming through. When there's action in the Denver metro area, they call me to arrange help and keep the place in order. That's fine when I'm there, but when I'm out on the road I have to do it remotely. It's not a problem, because I have good help in Denver. But the helpers can't drive trailers.

When I pulled into the yard I saw there were nine trailers dropped willy-nilly, all facing in different directions. All of them, I knew, would be full of empty cartons, garbage, and unfolded moving pads. The cleanup would be a massive job that reminded me of that chapter in *Moby-Dick* after a whale has been caught and killed and the oil has been boiled off. The whalemen spend several days cleaning the ship and themselves, from the bilges to the top of the mainmast. Once they're done, or sometimes in the middle of the job, they spot another whale and start the process all over again. Cleaning up a previously fully loaded trailer takes two men almost a full day. There are a couple hundred pads to fold, tape to take off, cartons to empty of paper, and trash to haul. Then it's off to the recycling center to dump the cardboard. If I have time, I'll hose out the trailers. It's hard to believe how filthy trailers can get hauling household goods. Not as bad as a chicken choker, but bad enough.

I called Julio and Carlos and told them we had a week's worth of cleanup. They weren't thrilled. First, I'd need to put some order in the lot, which meant I had to put the trailers in a line. I started with the one hooked to my tractor. I backed it onto the property line, set the brakes, laid down a sheet of plywood, and went around to the far side and cranked the trailer landing gear onto the plywood. I've set trailers down on dirt before, and sometimes the landing gear sinks down a couple of feet so the trailer looks like a cat stretching itself with forepaws low and ass in the air. (You need a heavy forklift or a tow truck to get the thing high enough to slip a tractor under when that happens.) After the landing gear was down I pulled off the gladhands that hold the service and brake hoses, and disconnected the electrical cord. Then I reached under and pulled the fifth-wheel lever, releasing the kingpin. (The fifth wheel is the roundish flat metal plate on the tractor that the trailer sits on. The kingpin is the rod that sticks down from the trailer that fits into a slot on the fifth wheel and locks the apparatus together.) Next, I climbed into the cab, released the air ride bags, thereby lowering my tractor, disengaged the air brake, and slid off the trailer. Now I was a bobtail tractor looking for a trailer. I backed up to another one to the point where my fifth wheel was just under the trailer. I set my brakes and hopped out to eyeball the levels to be sure they were about even. If I was too high, my fifth wheel would bang into the trailer body and damage it. If I was too low, the kingpin would bypass the fifth wheel, and my trailer would hit the back of my tractor and damage that. If I was only a little too low or a little too high, the fifth wheel hook wouldn't engage, so when I pulled away the trailer would drop onto the ground.

I've done this twice and it's horrible. The first time was on the Post Road in Cos Cob in my early days. I didn't check the coupling, and when I made the hard left from Cross Lane onto the main road the trailer slipped off, breaking the hoses and blocking all lanes of traffic. I'm very lucky I didn't kill anyone. The idea of traveling down a highway and watching the trailer slide away into an oncoming lane of traffic gives me nightmares even now. Especially now. Anyhow, when I dropped that one, John Callahan came out with a forklift and an extra set of hoses. He replaced the hoses, lifted the trailer with the forklift, and had Little Al slide the tractor underneath and hook up. An operation like that takes about twenty minutes, provided you have the forklift and hoses to hand.

The second time I did it was relatively recently, when a driver dropped a trailer at residence and I was to take it away. I checked the coupling and the hook was engaged, but when I started moving I could see the trailer sliding off in my mirror. I didn't bust the hoses that time, but I did have to spend a half hour cranking the landing gear all the way from the bottom. Nowadays I always have a flashlight with me, and once I hook up I go underneath the trailer and visually inspect the coupling. After that I set my trailer brake, put the tractor into low low gear, and engage the clutch. If the tractor doesn't move, I'm locked in, probably. I'm never 100 percent sure until I make a turn. It's nerve-racking.

After hooking up the next trailer, I lined it up next to mine, about a foot away. I needed to make this line tight. I did this eight more times, and I had a neat row of trailers. It took about two hours. It wasn't real moving work, like lifting pianos up staircases, but wasn't sipping coffee at the truckstop either. Nine times crank-ing up the landing gear, nine times cranking down the gear, thirty-six times into and out of the tractor, eighteen times coupling hoses, eighteen times connecting and disconnecting the gladhands, and nine times pulling fifth-wheel pins. And I hadn't started the day's work yet.

Since I had a whole week, I was going to wash out the trailers. I pulled the first one out of the line and opened all the doors.

There's a large set of double doors on the driver side and four sets of doors on the shotgun side. I parked next to the loading dock, and we tossed all the pads and cartons and garbage onto the dock. Julio had a pressure hose, and he started at the front washing out the ceiling, walls, and floor. A moving trailer has slotted sides, and you wouldn't believe the stuff that gets in there. Food, dust, dead mice, dirt, more food, and more dust. He moved the hose down the fifty-three feet and stopped at the end with his pile of yuck. We dumped it into a dumpster, and I drove the trailer around the block to dry it off. In the Colorado summer it takes about ten minutes for a trailer to dry out. Then the pads will be folded, the equipment stowed, and the cartons flattened for recycling. While the boys did that I performed a complete trailer inspection, starting on the ground with a mechanic's creeper to check the brake adjustments. Each trailer brake has an arm that engages the brake. The play in the arm shouldn't be more than an eighth of an inch. If it's too much or too little, I adjust them with a 7/16 wrench. Brake arms are touchy little buggers, and they have a tendency to lock up in cold weather. I've spent many an early morning underneath my trailer in the snow thawing frozen brake arms with a safety flare.

Next, I checked the trailer bubble, which is a small plastic compartment at the front of the trailer, for a current registration, current DOT inspection, and current insurance card. I took my tire wear gauge and checked the tread depth on all eight skins. I took my tire buddy, a wooden dowel with a metal handle (it makes a great weapon), and banged all the tires to check inflation. I can feel if a tire is flat or soft, and if it is, I make a note to inflate or replace it at the next truckstop. Then I checked all the doors for locks and made sure the locks were lubricated and all had the same key.

We could do two of these trailers in one long day, and I had ten to do.

I'm going into all of this in detail not just to sing my song about the work but to let shippers out there know what it entails to get a truck to your front door. If any of the things I'm checking needs attention, it's more work, time, and money. A new tire is $400 at the truckstop and a lot more if you're out on the Big Slab, plus hours of wasted time. A DOT inspection is $150 and at least a day if there's nothing that needs fixing, and something always needs fixing. It costs $125 to register the trailer, $1,000 to insure it, not including cargo, and $20,000 to properly equip it. My tractor costs $3,500 to register, $10,000 to insure, and $125,000 to replace. Everything requires an army of office workers doing accounting, insurance, and federal compliance in fuel taxes, registrations, logbooks, driver certification, drug testing, and DOT physical exams. Any compliance violation results in a shutdown of the vehicle.

After I'd finished with the trailers I was going to air out the mattresses in my sleeper, wash and vacuum the tractor interior, and stock the fridge with Gatorade and water. I do all this ahead of time so I don't get delayed getting to your job.

———

By Friday night I'd gotten the ten trailers and my tractor cleaned and ready. Call me a sentimental old mover, but after Carlos and Julio left at 9 p.m. it was still light out, so I cracked open a beer, unlocked each trailer, and looked inside to enjoy the handiwork. Rows and rows of clean, perfectly folded pads. Belly boxes filled with cargo bars and plywood of various widths. Equipment boxes with floor runners, straps, car tie-downs, bungee cords, shrink-wrap, door pads, and humpstraps. Each trailer was perfect, and I was ready to mess them up all over again.

I ran out of room in the lot for trailer number ten, but I was loading it the next day in Littleton for San Diego, so I parked it out on the street. That night a mini tornado howled through Erie and blew the rig over onto its side. I got a call from the state police at 11 p.m. asking if there was anybody inside. I told them no and went over to supervise the two tow trucks I hired to put the tractor-trailer back on its sneakers. I have a video of the truck being upended. It cost $2,000, and one of the tow trucks took my tractor to the shop. The whole left side had been crushed. No mirrors, no windows, no lights. The trailer doors had been sprung and the landing gear destroyed. That trailer never went back out on the road.

I got to bed at 1 a.m. and was up at 4 for the trip to Penske Truck Rental in Aurora. I arrived at 6, picked up a rental tractor, drove to Erie, hooked up another trailer, and arrived with my crew at the residence in Littleton at 8:30. As I walked up to the shipper, holding my card in my hand and a smile on my face, he looked at me and said:

"You're late."

ACKNOWLEDGMENTS

Thanks first and foremost to Matt Weiland at W. W. Norton, who believed in the book and in my ability to write it.

To Rafe Sagalyn, who took a proposal from an unknown trucker and managed to get Matt to look at it.

To Will Joyce, my lifelong friend, nemesis, hero, and villain.

To those who encouraged me in this project over the long years: Pam Murphy, Laura Byrne, Lori DeBoer, Sarah Massey-Warren, Deb Edgecombe, Betsy Crane, Wendy Hudson.

To Christopher Hunt for early edits, help on my proposal, and lots of mountain hikes talking about writing.

To Cait and Cullen Murphy for their encouragement and moral support.

To India Cooper, who showed me I should have paid more attention in seventh-grade grammar class. And to all the staff at W. W. Norton who welcomed me into the fold.